BAPTISTWAY ADULT BIBLE STUDY GUIDE®

The Book of Genesis

PEOPLE RELATING TO GOD

BRIAN HARBOUR
MEREDITH STONE
DON RANEY

BAPTISTWAYPRESS®

Dallas, Texas

The Book of Genesis: People Relating to God—BaptistWay Adult Bible Study Guide®

BAPTISTWAY PRESS® Management Team
Executive Director, Baptist General Convention of Texas: Randel Everett
Director, Education/Discipleship Center: Chris Liebrum
Director, Bible Study/Discipleship Team: Phil Miller
Publisher, BAPTISTWAY PRESS®: Ross West

Cover and Interior Design and Production: Desktop Miracles, Inc.
Printing: Data Reproductions Corporation

First edition: April 2010
ISBN–13: 978–1–934731–44–4

How to Make the Best Use of This Issue

Whether you're the teacher or a student—

1. Start early in the week before your class meets.

2. Overview the study. Review the table of contents and read the study introduction. Try to see how each lesson relates to the overall study.

3. Use your Bible to read and consider prayerfully the Scripture passages for the lesson. (You'll see that each writer has chosen a favorite translation for the lessons in this issue. You're free to use the Bible translation you prefer and compare it with the translation chosen for that unit, of course.)

4. After reading all the Scripture passages in your Bible, then read the writer's comments. The comments are intended to be an aid to your study of the Bible.

5. Read the small articles—"sidebars"—in each lesson. They are intended to provide additional, enrichment information and inspiration and to encourage thought and application.

6. Try to answer for yourself the questions included in each lesson. They're intended to encourage further thought and application, and they can also be used in the class session itself.

If you're the teacher—

A. Do all of the things just mentioned, of course. As you begin the study with your class, be sure to find a way to help your class know the date on which each lesson will be studied. You might do this in one or more of the following ways:

   • In the first session of the study, briefly overview the study by identifying with your class the date on which each lesson will be studied. Lead your class to write the date in the table of contents on page 7 and on the first page of each lesson.

- Make and post a chart that indicates the date on which each lesson will be studied.
- If all of your class has e-mail, send them an e-mail with the dates the lessons will be studied.
- Provide a bookmark with the lesson dates. You may want to include information about your church and then use the bookmark as an outreach tool, too. A model for a bookmark can be downloaded from www.baptistwaypress.org on the Resources for Adults page.
- Develop a sticker with the lesson dates, and place it on the table of contents or on the back cover.

B. Get a copy of the *Teaching Guide*, a companion piece to this *Study Guide*. The *Teaching Guide* contains additional Bible comments plus two teaching plans. The teaching plans in the *Teaching Guide* are intended to provide practical, easy-to-use teaching suggestions that will work in your class.

C. After you've studied the Bible passage, the lesson comments, and other material, use the teaching suggestions in the *Teaching Guide* to help you develop your plan for leading your class in studying each lesson.

D. You may want to get the additional adult Bible study comments—*Adult Online Bible Commentary*—by Dr. Jim Denison (president, The Center for Informed Faith, and theologian-in-residence, Baptist General Convention of Texas) that are available at www.baptistwaypress.org and can be downloaded free. An additional teaching plan plus teaching resource items are also available at www.baptistwaypress.org.

E. You also may want to get the enrichment teaching help that is provided on the internet by the *Baptist Standard* at www.baptiststandard.com. (Other class participants may find this information helpful, too.) Call 214–630–4571 to begin your subscription to the printed or electronic edition of the *Baptist Standard*.

F. Enjoy leading your class in discovering the meaning of the Scripture passages and in applying these passages to their lives.

Writers of This Study Guide

Brian Harbour wrote unit one, lessons one through three. After serving as a pastor for forty-two years, Dr. Harbour retired to give his attention to writing and teaching. He is president of SeminaryPLUS, a non-profit organization that provides coaching and encouragement to pastors. He also serves as an adjunct professor at Dallas Baptist University and as Visiting Professor in Religion at Baylor University.

Meredith Stone wrote lessons four through six. Rev. Stone is teaching pastor at Crosspoint Fellowship, Abilene, Texas. She also serves as coordinator of recruitment for Logsdon Seminary and has taught adjunctively for Hardin-Simmons in the areas of Old Testament and Hebrew. She is a graduate of Hardin-Simmons University (B.A., M.A.) and is working toward a Ph.D. in Biblical Interpretation at Brite Divinity School.

Don Raney wrote lessons seven and eight in unit two. Dr. Raney is pastor of First Baptist Church, Petersburg, Texas. He is a graduate of the University of Alabama (B.A.). He received his Ph.D. in Old Testament from Southwestern Baptist Theological Seminary, Fort Worth, Texas.

The Book of Genesis: People Relating to God

DATE OF STUDY

UNIT ONE

Beginning at the Beginning

UNIT TWO

Onward with God

Introducing

THE BOOK OF GENESIS:
People Relating to God

Overviewing the Study

This study combines two significant and attractive ways of studying Scripture—studying a book of the Bible and studying the people in the book of the Bible. The study moves through the Book of Genesis, following the book's contours and seeking to connect each lesson in a vital manner to the main truths of the book. It does this by focusing on key figures in Genesis so that each lesson contains biographical insights while emphasizing major truths seen in the character being studied.

Another feature that lends promise to this study is that it's on the Book of Genesis, truly a foundational book of the Bible. The book begins with the words "in the beginning" (Genesis 1:1) and concludes with someone named Joseph dying and "being placed in a coffin in Egypt" (Gen. 50:26).[1] Clearly much happens between those two phrases. After the words "in the beginning," the book proceeds to tell of God as Creator; of Adam and Eve's being dismissed from Paradise; of Cain's tragic conflict with Abel; and of God's becoming dissatisfied with human beings' way of living and graciously making a fresh start with Noah. The actions in Genesis 1—11 take place on the broad, worldwide stage, often without specific connections to a recognizable place. The emphasis in these beginning chapters of Genesis seems to be more on conveying foundational truths than on filling in all the details of the surroundings.

With Genesis 12, the details start to appear more definite and more recognizable. The focus is sharpened considerably. In Genesis 12, the focus narrows from the broad world to one man, who would found one people. This focusing of the biblical story occurs because God wanted to use that one man and one people to reach and bless *all* people. God promised Abram, "I will make of you a great nation, and I will bless you, and make your name great, so that you will be a blessing. I will bless those who bless you, and the one who curses you I will curse; and in you all the families of the earth shall be blessed" (Gen. 12:2–3). The rest of Genesis focuses on the outworking and preservation of that magnificent promise through four generations—the generations of Abraham, Isaac, Jacob, and Joseph.

Although Joseph died and "was placed in a coffin in Egypt" (50:26), the story of God's promise didn't end there. As Joseph himself said to his brothers not long before his death, "God will surely come to you, and bring you up out of this land to the land that he swore to Abraham, to Isaac, and to Jacob" (50:24). The next book, Exodus, tells how God did that. In fact, the rest of the Bible builds on Genesis and tells the further story of how God worked out in history the promise to Abraham that ". . . all the families of the earth shall be blessed" (Gen. 12:3).

Why the Shorter-than-Usual Study

This study of the Book of Genesis is shorter than our usual BaptistWay® studies. It's eight sessions instead of the regular thirteen or fourteen. Why? The main reason the study is structured in this way is that our immediately previous study on the Gospel of Luke was a longer-than-usual study. Thus a briefer study was needed in order to return to our regular publication schedule. As it has worked out, providing only eight sessions for this study of Genesis enables us to provide eight lessons on seven strong biblical characters in Genesis.[2]

It's About the People

The Book of Genesis can be outlined with two main points—the broad, foundational view of God's working with people as portrayed in Genesis 1—11; and the focused view that begins with God's call to Abraham in Genesis 12 and extends through Joseph in Genesis 50.

Unit one, "Beginning at the Beginning," consists of three lessons from Genesis 1—11. These lessons are on Adam and Eve in Genesis 3; Cain and Abel in Genesis 4; and Noah in Genesis 6—9.

Unit two, "Onward with God," contains five lessons from Genesis 12—50. These lessons trace the beginnings of God's focus on Israel as the way in which God would bring blessing to all people. Included in this unit are lessons on Abraham (from Gen. 12; 15; 17); Sarah (from Gen. 18; 21); Jacob (from Gen. 25; 27; 32; 35); and Joseph (two lessons from Gen. 37—50).

UNIT ONE: BEGINNING AT THE BEGINNING

Lesson 1	Adam and Eve: All About "I"	Genesis 3
Lesson 2	Cain and Abel: Who Cares?	Genesis 4:1–16
Lesson 3	Noah: Finding Grace	Genesis 6:5–9; 7:1–6; 8:13–22

UNIT TWO: ONWARD WITH GOD

Lesson 4	Abraham: Following By Faith	Genesis 11:31—12:7; 15:1–6; 17:1–8
Lesson 5	Sarah: Laughing At God's Promise	Genesis 18:1–15; 21:1–7
Lesson 6	Jacob: Deception and Blessing	Genesis 25:21–34; 27:22–36b; 32:22–32; 35:9–12
Lesson 7	Joseph: Tempted But Faithful	Genesis 39
Lesson 8	Joseph: Participating in God's Purpose	Genesis 45:1–15; 50:19–21, 24

Additional Resources for Studying *Genesis: People Relating to God*[3]

Bill T. Arnold. *Genesis.* The New Cambridge Bible Commentary. Cambridge: Cambridge University Press, 2009.

Walter Brueggemann. *Genesis.* Interpretation, A Bible Commentary for Teaching and Preaching. Atlanta: John Knox Press, 1982.

Terence Fretheim. "The Book of Genesis." *The New Interpreter's Bible.* Volume 1. Nashville: Abingdon Press, 1994.

Victor P. Hamilton. *The Book of Genesis: Chapters 1—17.* The New International Commentary on the Old Testament. Grand Rapids, Michigan: William B. Eerdmans Publishing Company, 1990.

Victor P. Hamilton. *The Book of Genesis: Chapters 18—50*. The New International Commentary on the Old Testament. Grand Rapids, Michigan: William B. Eerdmans Publishing Company, 1995.

Gerhard von Rad. *Genesis. A Commentary.* Revised Edition. Translated by John H. Marks. The Old Testament Library. Philadelphia: Westminster Press, 1972.

Gordon J. Wenham. *Genesis 1—15*. Word Biblical Commentary. Volume 1. Waco, Texas: Word Books, Publisher, 1987.

Claus Westermann. *Genesis 12—36: A Commentary.* Translated by John J. Scullion. Minneapolis: Augsburg Publishing House, 1985.

Claus Westermann. *Genesis 37—50: A Commentary.* Translated by John J. Scullion. Minneapolis: Augsburg Publishing House, 1986.

NOTES

1. Unless otherwise indicated, all Scripture quotations in "Introducing the Book of Genesis: People Relating to God" are from the New Revised Standard Version.

2. A thirteen-session study of Genesis 12—50 is also available from BAPTISTWAY PRESS®. See *Genesis 12—50: Family Matters* on our order form or at www.baptistwaypress.org.

3. Listing a book does not imply full agreement by the writers or BAPTISTWAY PRESS® with all of its comments.

Beginning at the Beginning

Genesis is undeniably one of the most important books in the Bible and for a number of reasons. Every great theological doctrine of the faith can be traced back to the story told in Genesis, giving the Book of Genesis theological importance. Genesis is also important because it describes the origin of the most basic elements of life today, including the home; work; languages and ethnic diversity; human sin; and the purpose of God for humanity. Too, Genesis has historical importance because this book covers more history than all the remainder of the Bible together, and the writer of Genesis reveals the origin of the conflicts that still rage between nations today.

Genesis 1—11 provides a general description of God's original creation and explains how humanity distorted God's original plan. Then, the remainder of the Book of Genesis describes God's selection of Israel as his agent to redeem humanity and restore the world to its proper course. Genesis develops the story around the lives of people whose names have become almost universally known: Adam and Eve, Cain and Abel, and Noah in the first section of Genesis (Genesis 1—11); and Abraham, Sarah, Isaac, Jacob, and Joseph in the remainder of the book (Gen. 12—50).

The story in Genesis is not ordinary history. The story is selective rather than exhaustive, and not just factual but also interpretive. The Bible is not a history of humankind but is instead the story of God's unfolding plan for humankind. Therefore, the biblical writers gave priority to personalities and events that bore directly on the purpose of God.

Too, the story in Genesis is not intended as a scientific treatise. The biblical writer used that day's understanding of the nature of the universe but poured eternal truth about God and humanity into that understanding. The result is that the truth of the story persists despite the changed understanding of the world and the universe since that time. The purpose of the Book of Genesis is to give an account of the origin of all things as the backdrop against which the story of God's chosen people can be told.[1]

UNIT ONE: BEGINNING AT THE BEGINNING

NOTES

1. Unless otherwise indicated, all Scripture translations in unit 1, lessons 1–3, are from the New International Version.

FOCAL TEXT
Genesis 3

BACKGROUND
Genesis 2:4—3:24

MAIN IDEA

Disastrous consequences occur when people reject God's call to live in God's world in faithfulness to God.

QUESTION TO EXPLORE

How are you anxiously trying to meet your perceived needs rather than living in faithful trust in God?

STUDY AIM

To relate the account of Adam and Eve to my choices about whether to live in faithfulness to God or in self-centeredness

QUICK READ

By following their own desires instead of obeying God's commands, Adam and Eve started humanity down a pathway toward personal destruction and alienation from God.

LESSON ONE
Adam and Eve: All About "I"

Have you ever been in a situation that suddenly shifted from advantageous to disastrous? You were on top of the world one moment and then in the next moment the bottom dropped out from under you.

That is what happened to Adam and Eve. Genesis 2 ends with Adam and Eve in an ideal situation. Created in God's image for fellowship with him, Adam and Eve basked in the glow of that divine companionship. Created with a relationship hunger within, Adam and Eve satisfied that relationship hunger in their companionship with each other. Created with some basic needs for physical nourishment, Adam and Eve gratified that hunger with the luscious fruit of the garden. They were in an ideal situation.

In contrast, Genesis 3 ends with Adam and Eve in an absolute mess. Adam and Eve cowered behind a tree so they would not have to face God. Gone was their amiable fellowship with God. Their once cordial relationship was now strained. Then God kicked them out of their garden paradise. They were in a mess.

What happened? The biblical writer answers that question by describing in Genesis 3 Adam and Eve's disobedience to God's specific commands about how they were to conduct themselves in the Garden. We refer to the event described in our text as the fall of humanity. By their disobedience, Adam and Eve introduced sin into human history.

GENESIS 3

¹ Now the serpent was more crafty than any of the wild animals the LORD God had made. He said to the woman, "Did God really say, 'You must not eat from any tree in the garden'?"

² The woman said to the serpent, "We may eat fruit from the trees in the garden, ³ but God did say, 'You must not eat fruit from the tree that is in the middle of the garden, and you must not touch it, or you will die.'"

⁴ "You will not surely die," the serpent said to the woman. ⁵ "For God knows that when you eat of it your eyes will be opened, and you will be like God, knowing good and evil."

⁶ When the woman saw that the fruit of the tree was good for food and pleasing to the eye, and also desirable for gaining wisdom, she took some and ate it. She also gave some to her

husband, who was with her, and he ate it. ⁷Then the eyes of both of them were opened, and they realized they were naked; so they sewed fig leaves together and made coverings for themselves.

⁸Then the man and his wife heard the sound of the LORD God as he was walking in the garden in the cool of the day, and they hid from the LORD God among the trees of the garden. ⁹But the LORD God called to the man, "Where are you?"

¹⁰He answered, "I heard you in the garden, and I was afraid because I was naked; so I hid."

¹¹And he said, "Who told you that you were naked? Have you eaten from the tree that I commanded you not to eat from?"

¹²The man said, "The woman you put here with me—she gave me some fruit from the tree, and I ate it."

¹³Then the LORD God said to the woman, "What is this you have done?"

The woman said, "The serpent deceived me, and I ate."

¹⁴So the LORD God said to the serpent, "Because you have done this,

"Cursed are you above all the livestock
and all the wild animals!
You will crawl on your belly
and you will eat dust
all the days of your life.
¹⁵And I will put enmity
between you and the woman,
and between your offspring and hers;
he will crush your head,
and you will strike his heel."
¹⁶To the woman he said,
"I will greatly increase your pains in childbearing;
with pain you will give birth to children.
Your desire will be for your husband,
and he will rule over you."
¹⁷To Adam he said, "Because you listened to your wife and ate from the tree about which I commanded
you, 'You must not eat of it,'
"Cursed is the ground because of you;

through painful toil you will eat of it
all the days of your life.
¹⁸ It will produce thorns and thistles for you,
and you will eat the plants of the field.
¹⁹ By the sweat of your brow
you will eat your food
until you return to the ground,
since from it you were taken;
for dust you are
and to dust you will return."
²⁰ Adam named his wife Eve, because she would become the mother of all the living.
²¹ The Lᴏʀᴅ God made garments of skin for Adam and his wife and clothed them. ²² And the Lᴏʀᴅ God said, "The man has now become like one of us, knowing good and evil. He must not be allowed to reach out his hand and take also from the tree of life and eat, and live forever." ²³ So the Lᴏʀᴅ God banished him from the Garden of Eden to work the ground from which he had been taken. ²⁴ After he drove the man out, he placed on the east side of the Garden of Eden cherubim and a flaming sword flashing back and forth to guard the way to the tree of life.

The Act (3:1–6)

As Genesis 3 opens, temptation appeared in the form of a "serpent" (Genesis 3:1). The serpent was a real animal. Perhaps that is what intrigued Eve at first, because she heard an animal speak, revealing a rational power she did not know animals had. Later references identify the serpent with Satan (Revelation 12:9) and reveal that Satan used the serpent to tempt humanity.

Although Satan was obviously behind the temptations presented by the serpent, Adam and Eve could not blame their fall on the presence of temptation. Temptation simply provided the opportunity for sin. Adam and Eve's deliberate choice actualized the sin.

Notice the successive steps in the actualization of sin. The first step down the pathway to disobedience is curiosity. Satan spoke to Eve through the serpent (Gen. 3:1), an animal that ordinarily did not speak. Satan used this unusual event to arouse Eve's curiosity.

Satan then pushed Eve's curiosity in the direction of doubt. Satan's question seemed innocent enough: "Did God really say, 'You must not eat from any tree in the garden'?" (3:1). Yet, that question aroused suspicion concerning God's intentions. Satan led Eve to doubt God's love (3:1). He then persuaded Eve to doubt God's honesty with the exclamation, "You will not surely die" (3:4). He then motivated Eve to doubt God's goodness with the explanation, "For God knows that when you eat of it your eyes will be opened, and you will be like God, knowing good and evil" (3:5). Curiosity and doubt finally prompted the act of disobedience. Eve ate the fruit and then gave some to Adam (3:6).

The Accountability (3:7–13)

This act of disobedience instantly transformed all of Adam and Eve's relationships. Sin altered their relationship with each other. Genesis 2:25 declares that "they felt no shame" at their nakedness, reflecting complete

---

SATAN

The Bible uses different names to identify Satan. He is called "the god of this age" (2 Corinthians 4:4), "an angel of light" (2 Cor. 11:14), and our "enemy" (1 Peter 5:8). Matthew's Gospel calls him "the tempter" (Matthew 4:3) and "the devil" (Matt. 4:1). The most common name for him is Satan (1 Chronicles 21:1; Job 1:6; John 13:27; Acts 5:3).

The biblical writers make it clear that Satan wants to "devour" or destroy us (1 Pet. 5:8). In the Old Testament, Satan led God's people to presumption in 1 Chronicles 21:1, slandered God's people to God's face in Zechariah 3:1, and accused Job in Job 1:10–11. In the New Testament, Satan tempted Jesus in Matthew 3, influenced Judas to betray Jesus in John 13:2, and filled the heart of Ananias and led him to lie to the church in Acts 5:3. Satan continues today using every method he can to discourage the people of God, discredit the word of God, and derail the work of God.

openness toward each other. After their sin, Adam and Eve were embarrassed by their nakedness and immediately felt compelled to cover that nakedness from each other (3:7).

Even more serious, their sin changed their relationship with God. Created in God's image for fellowship with him, Adam and Eve previously enjoyed a warm and cordial relationship with God. After their sin, they sought to avoid seeing God by hiding behind a tree in the Garden (3:8). Instinctively, they realized that God knew what they had done, and they did not want to face their own accountability. God demanded a response from the creatures he had made for fellowship with him. Adam admitted that they were uncomfortable with each other's nakedness and that they were afraid of facing God. God responded more with a question than an accusation. He asked whether they had disobeyed his command and eaten the forbidden fruit.

At that point, the blame game began. Adam refused to accept responsibility for his disobedience. Instead, he blamed Eve. He pointed his finger at "the woman you put here with me" (3:12). Eve also refused to accept responsibility for her disobedience. Instead, she blamed the serpent. She pointed her finger at the serpent and explained, "The serpent deceived me" (3:13). They sound like the little boy who justified his fight at school by explaining to his parents, "The fight started when Billy hit me back."

God rejected Adam and Eve's attempt to escape culpability. He countered their excuses with the clear accusation: "Because you have done this" (3:14). God held both Adam and Eve to be guilty. In the passage that follows, as God explained the consequences of their disobedience, God addressed both Adam and Eve.

The Aftermath (3:14–24)

What happened when Adam and Eve yielded to temptation and sinned against God? First we see the personal consequences. Sin introduced guilt for the first time into human consciousness (3:7). Adam and Eve knew they had done something wrong. That awareness, which they attempted to hide behind their excuses, generated the guilt. Their guilt in turn created a fear of facing God. No longer did they welcome God's presence in the Garden. Instead, they hid from God's presence.

Their disobedience disrupted God's plan for their daily lives and distorted their relationship with each other. God's declaration beginning in Genesis 3:14 is not a prescription but rather a description. God did not prescribe in this verse the kind of life he wanted for humanity. Instead, God described the distorted life humanity would experience as a result of their sin.

God first addressed Satan, in the form of the serpent (3:14–16). Satan might believe that he won an enduring victory over humanity that would permanently disrupt God's plan. God reminded Satan that ultimately he would be crushed by the heel of one who is the offspring of Adam and Eve (3:15). Theologians call this verse the *protoevangelium*, meaning *the first gospel*. God offered a promise of ultimate victory in the midst of humanity's greatest defeat. The serpent represented Satan. The "offspring" of the woman was a reference to Christ. On the cross, Satan would bruise the Messiah, striking "his heel." In the resurrection, the risen Messiah would crush Satan and deal a death blow to Satan's cause.

God then addressed Eve (3:16). He promised suffering in childbirth and submission in her relationship with her husband. This was not God's original plan. God clarified his original intention and permanent plan for the relationship between men and women in the creation account when he spoke of both man and woman as being in the image of God (1:26–27) and when he spoke of Eve as Adam's "helper suitable for him" (2:18). The word for "helper" is the same word biblical writers use for God in at least three places: Exodus 18:4; Deuteronomy 33:29; and Hosea 13:9. In other words, as God was a "helper" for humanity, woman was to

---

A QUESTION FROM THE CONVENIENCE STORE

When you check out at the convenience store, the clerk owes you three dollars and twenty cents in change. The clerk hands you your change. You take it without looking at it carefully. As you get to your car, you start to put the money into your billfold. As you do, you notice that the clerk evidently gave you a twenty and two one-dollar bills instead of three one-dollar bills. What do you do? Do you keep the money or do you return it?

be for man. This hardly reflects a subordinate role. In Genesis 3:16, the suffering of childbirth for woman and her subordination to man were not God's plan but instead distorted God's plan.

Finally, God addressed Adam (Gen. 3:17–19). God promised that disappointment and hardship would come from his labor. God also announced the fulfillment of his earlier warning—that eating from the fruit of the forbidden treat would result in death (2:17). Life on earth would not be eternal, but instead humanity would return to the dust from which they came.

God mixed judgment with compassion in his final actions in response to humanity's disobedience (3:20–24). He removed Adam and Eve from the Garden so they would not eat of the tree of life and live forever in this distorted human condition caused by their disobedience. God also clothed them, to provide protection and to alleviate their discomfort caused by their disobedience.

Adam and Eve's disobedience altered forever their relationship with each other and with God. Yet, their disobedience did not ultimately disrupt God's plan for humanity. What the first Adam undid would be repaired by the new Adam. As Paul put it in one of his letters to the Corinthians: "For as in Adam all die, so in Christ all will be made alive" (1 Corinthians 15:22).

Applying the Lesson to Life

This foundational story in the Bible reminds us of some important truths for today. To begin with, Genesis 3 reminds us that temptation is merely the opportunity to sin, not sin itself. Second, the story acknowledges that each of us stands where Adam and Eve stood, having to decide between following our own selfish desires or being obedient to God's command. Further, the story uncovers some of the tricks Satan uses to deceive us and lead us astray. The story also affirms that each of us is responsible for our own decisions. We cannot point the finger of blame at anyone but ourselves. Finally, the story reveals God's grace. Even as God kicked Adam and Eve out of the Garden, God provided clothes for them to wear and gave them the promise of ultimate victory.

QUESTIONS

1. What is the danger of confusing the distinction between temptation and sin?

2. Why do you think Satan approached Eve in the form of a serpent?

3. What similarities can you identify between the method Satan used to tempt Adam and Eve to sin and the methods he uses on you?

4. Whom do we blame today when we make wrong choices and sin against God?

5. What are some consequences of human sin?

FOCAL TEXT
Genesis 4:1–16

BACKGROUND
Genesis 4

MAIN IDEA
People who wish to have a right relationship with God must also have a caring relationship with other people.

QUESTION TO EXPLORE
In what ways are we causing harm to our fellow human beings rather than extending care to them?

STUDY AIM
To identify ways I need to extend care to my fellow human beings, including my family, rather than causing harm to them

QUICK READ
Provoked by his disappointment with God and his resentment of his brother, Cain murdered his brother and demonstrated that families have been dysfunctional from the beginning of human history.

LESSON TWO
Cain and Abel: Who Cares?

Nowhere in life is there such a gap between what we expect and what we actually experience as in our family life. The myth of the white picket fence still prevails in the minds of many people as they approach marriage and establish their new home. They look for a perfect mate with whom they can establish a perfect marriage that will produce perfect children and will provide perfect fulfillment. We do not have to look far or listen long to realize that most homes do not turn out like that.

We have a name for what happens in most of our homes today. We call them *dysfunctional families.* After a lifetime of studying God's word and working with families, I have reached the conclusion that every family is dysfunctional to a degree.

Even when we go back to the beginning and study the first families that existed, we recognize this truth. The first family of Adam and Eve and their sons Cain and Abel did not enjoy perfect harmony. Instead, one brother murdered another brother. Their story has been relived by many other dysfunctional families across the centuries. Let us take a closer look at this first family of the Bible.

GENESIS 4:1–16

[1] Adam lay with his wife Eve, and she became pregnant and gave birth to Cain. She said, "With the help of the LORD I have brought forth a man." [2] Later she gave birth to his brother Abel.

Now Abel kept flocks, and Cain worked the soil. [3] In the course of time Cain brought some of the fruits of the soil as an offering to the LORD. [4] But Abel brought fat portions from some of the firstborn of his flock. The LORD looked with favor on Abel and his offering, [5] but on Cain and his offering he did not look with favor. So Cain was very angry, and his face was downcast.

[6] Then the LORD said to Cain, "Why are you angry? Why is your face downcast? [7] If you do what is right, will you not be accepted? But if you do not do what is right, sin is crouching at your door; it desires to have you, but you must master it."

[8] Now Cain said to his brother Abel, "Let's go out to the field." And while they were in the field, Cain attacked his brother Abel and killed him.

[9] Then the LORD said to Cain, "Where is your brother Abel?"

"I don't know," he replied. "Am I my brother's keeper?"

¹⁰ The LORD said, "What have you done? Listen! Your brother's blood cries out to me from the ground. ¹¹ Now you are under a curse and driven from the ground, which opened its mouth to receive your brother's blood from your hand. ¹² When you work the ground, it will no longer yield its crops for you. You will be a restless wanderer on the earth."

¹³ Cain said to the LORD, "My punishment is more than I can bear. ¹⁴ Today you are driving me from the land, and I will be hidden from your presence; I will be a restless wanderer on the earth, and whoever finds me will kill me."

¹⁵ But the LORD said to him, "Not so; if anyone kills Cain, he will suffer vengeance seven times over." Then the LORD put a mark on Cain so that no one who found him would kill him. ¹⁶ So Cain went out from the LORD's presence and lived in the land of Nod, east of Eden.

The First Family (4:1–2)

The biblical writer painted the portrait of this first family with an economy of brush strokes. Our curiosity longs for more details about the ongoing relationship between Adam and Eve and how they handled their new environment and the new conditions surrounding them following their expulsion from the Garden. How did Adam and Eve pass their days? What kind of shelter did they live in? What did they look like? What did they eat? The biblical writer omitted these peripheral details and simply announced the central event around which the story unfolds—the birth of two brothers and the consequent conflict between them.

From the beginning of family life, marriage included the sexual dimension that Paul later described as the husband's "marital duty to his wife, and likewise the wife to her husband" (1 Corinthians 7:3). God provided sexual intercourse as the method by which Adam and Eve—and all of humanity after them—would fulfill his command to "be fruitful and increase in number" (Genesis 1:28). Following God's method, Eve became pregnant and gave birth to her first son, whom the first parents named Cain. Eve's response, "With the help of the LORD I have brought forth a man," seems to be a play on words. Originally, God had brought forth Eve out of a man by using his rib. Now, she would return the favor and a man would be brought forth out of a woman. This first birth was followed by a second birth as Adam and Eve also produced Abel.

The text does not give us the time frame on the birth of these two boys, and so we do not know the age gap between them. Instead, the passage focuses on the gap in their interests and abilities. Abel kept the flocks. He focused his attention on animals and provided for their care. In contrast, Cain worked the soil. He focused his attention on plants and nourished the soil to produce his crops. Like every family that follows them, this first family was marked by differences that would soon erupt into conflict.

The First Murder (4:3–8)

Again, the text gives few background facts about the conflict that led to the first murder in human history. "In the course of time" is an indefinite descriptive phrase. Both Cain and Abel seem to be adults at this point. Their clash grew out of their distinctive acts of worship as they brought their offerings to God. What motivated them to bring these thank offerings is not clear from the text. Nor did God seem to give them any prior instructions on how they were to carry out this act of worship. Each brother spontaneously brought an offering to the Lord out of the context of his own life. Cain, who worked the soil, naturally brought as his offering something he had grown. Abel, who watched over flocks, naturally brought as his offering an animal over which he had cared. Yet, God approved of Abel's offering but not Cain's.

Mystery clouds the story, for we cannot discern from the text why God favored Abel's offering over Cain's. Some commentators find the solution to this mystery in the descriptive phrase concerning Abel's sacrifice. The Bible says that Abel brought fat portions from "the firstborn" of his flock (Gen. 4:4). In contrast, Cain simply brought "some of the fruits" (4:3). Thus one view is that God commended Abel's offering over Cain's because Abel gave God his best while Cain simply gave whatever he happened to have at the time. Others find the solution to this mystery in

Hebrews 11:4, which explained the difference in this way: "By faith Abel offered God a better sacrifice than Cain did. By faith he was commended as a righteous man, when God spoke well of his offerings." Apparently God rejected Cain because of the spirit with which he gave his gift, and God accepted Abel's gift because his heart was right with God. Only Abel presented his offering "by faith." Jude 11 confirmed this conclusion when it identified "the way of Cain" with self-will and unbelief.

Equally mysterious is the question of how God indicated his favor on Abel and his disfavor on Cain. The most common explanation focuses on later demonstrations of God's favor. For example, in 1 Kings 18:38 God revealed his favor on Elijah's offering by sending a fire from heaven that "burned up the sacrifice, the wood, the stones and the soil, and also licked up the water in the trench." In 1 Chronicles 21:26, God revealed his favor on David's offering by sending "fire from heaven on the altar of burnt offering." Perhaps God demonstrated his favor on Abel's offering in similar fashion.

Leaving these peripheral questions unsolved, the text in Genesis focuses instead on the central event—the conflict between Cain and

SACRIFICES

Sacrifices played a vital part in the religious expression of the Old Testament. This practice of offering a sacrifice to God began with Cain and Abel, but we do not see a code to regulate sacrificial practice until later. When God gave Moses instructions for the construction of the tabernacle, he also provided instructions for sacrifices.

The regulations of the Old Testament called for a number of different offerings (see Leviticus 1—7). Let me mention three of these. Burnt offerings required the sacrifice by fire of a certain animal and would be offered for a variety of reasons, including a desire to honor God (Lev. 1). Grain offerings were to be offered from the harvest of the land to express gratitude for God's blessings (Lev. 2). Sin offerings were designated to deal with sins that were unintentionally committed (Lev. 4). No offering would cover intentional sins. In such cases, one had to throw oneself on the mercy of God. Cain and Abel thus inaugurated a practice that runs its way throughout the Old Testament.

Abel that led to Abel's death. Cain clearly understood that God favored Abel's offering over his, and he reacted with rage. What drew God's disfavor was not what Cain offered in sacrifice but how he offered it. Cain offered his sacrifice with reluctant spirit, grudgingly, and as an attempt to cover up his distrust toward God. God was not interested in sacrifices offered in that spirit and with that motive. God informed Cain that a change of approach and attitude on his part would solve the problem.

Cain, however, sought to solve the problem in another way. As we so often do, instead of recognizing that the problem is within ourselves, Cain projected the problem onto his brother. *It is not my fault*, perhaps he mumbled to himself. *It is Abel's fault*. (He apparently learned that strategy for conflict management from his parents. See lesson 1 on Gen. 3.) Since Abel seemed to be the problem in Cain's view, Cain chose to remove the source of the problem as he saw it by taking Abel's life.

Judgment and Grace (4:9–16)

In response to the first murder, God displayed both judgment and grace. The judgment came first (4:9–14). Unlike his parents when God confronted them with their earlier sin, Cain had no one to whom to pass the blame. Instead, he responded with indifference, denying that he should have any concern for his brother's well being. God's remarks surely reminded Cain that he was indeed his brother's keeper and that his act of misdirected vengeance on his brother violated this sacred responsibility.

TO APPLY THIS PASSAGE TO YOUR LIFE

- Accept the fact that your family, like every family, is dysfunctional to some degree
- Inventory the relationships within your family
- Identify any of these relationships that are generating a high level of tension or anger
- Determine some ways in which you can diffuse that tension
- Pray for God's wisdom

God pronounced a two-fold curse on Cain (Gen. 4:11–12). First, he would have to live a life of toil and strife as he tried to bring forth fruitfulness from what would remain for him a barren earth. For Adam, the soil would begrudgingly provide fruit for his labor (3:17–19). For Cain, the ground would be completely barren. Consequently, Cain would not be able to farm the land. Instead, he would be cursed to a life of wandering. He would never be able to settle in one place. He would never have a place where he could find the solace and stability of his own home. He was cursed to a life of wandering.

Cain gave his own interpretation to this curse from God. He interpreted the curse as a forced separation from the presence and protection of God (4:13–14). Cain complained that he was hidden from God's presence. Too, as he wandered around the earth, from one temporary resting place to another, Cain believed he would also be outside the care and protection of God. Therefore, he feared for his life.

God corrected Cain's supposition with a word of grace. Even though Cain would experience God's judgment, he would not be completely outside the protection of God's love. God promised to put "a mark on Cain" so no one would harm him (4:15). Since the text does not specify what this "mark" is, speculation has run wild. Some suggest that Cain was a paralytic. Others suggest that God put some mark on his forehead, perhaps the first letter of *Yahweh's* name. Still others believe this sign was something given to Cain to provide assurance, much like the rainbow was given later as a sign (9:12–17). Whatever the sign, it was a symbol of God's mercy and grace. In mercy, God did not give Cain what he deserved. In grace, God gave Cain what he did not deserve.

Despite this flash of grace, Cain still had to suffer the consequences of his action. As a result of Cain's sin, God relegated him to a lifetime of wandering "in the land of Nod" (4:16). The word "Nod" simply means *to wander* and perhaps is not meant to designate a place as much as it is to describe Cain's lifestyle. This term announced Cain's permanent separation from the first family of which he had been a part.

Applying the Lesson to Life

This story of the first murder reminds us of some important truths for today. To begin with, the story tells us something about our relationship with God. God not only demands that we give him our best. He also requires that we give him our best in the right way and with the right spirit.

The story also tells us something about the family. The intimacy of relationships within the family can generate a higher level of anger than any other human relationships. Consequently, we need to create ground rules for how we work through the conflicts that inevitably arise in the family.

Further, the story reminds us of our sacred responsibility to care for our fellow human beings rather than to harm them. We are to live the law of love in our relationships with other people (see Deuteronomy 6:5; Leviticus 19:18; Matthew 22:37–40).

Finally, the story reminds us that we are accountable for our actions. Cain somehow felt he could murder his brother and not experience any consequences in his life. He discovered the law of consequences that is woven through human history. Sin sets into motion a series of consequences that not only affects us but also those who are connected to us.

QUESTIONS

1. Why do you think God accepted Abel's offering but not Cain's?

2. In what ways does this passage apply to your family?

3. How would you answer Cain's retort to God: "Am I my brother's keeper?"

4. Can you think of a time when you gave God less than your best?

5. What part of the Scripture passage is most difficult for you to apply to yourself?

FOCAL TEXT
Genesis 6:5–9; 7:1–6; 8:13–22

BACKGROUND
Genesis 6:5—9:17

MAIN IDEA
God acts with grace and
mercy even in the midst
of bringing judgment on
people's wickedness.

QUESTION TO EXPLORE
Why do good things happen?

STUDY AIM
To state what God's actions
in relation to Noah reveal
about God and to identify
ways in which I observe
God's continued care in
spite of human evil

QUICK READ
God balanced judgment
on humanity with a
manifestation of grace as God
called, spared, and directed
Noah and his family.

LESSON THREE
Noah: Finding Grace

The law of consequences is a basic principle of life. Hollywood screen-writers and popular novelists have reflected on this theme across the years. Some people call it the *echo effect*. Paul captured this principle in his succinct statement to the Galatian Christians: "a man reaps what he sows" (Galatians 6:7). The psalmist even more graphically proclaimed this universal principle of life: "He who digs a hole and scoops it out falls into the pit he has made" (Psalm 7:15).

That is precisely what happened to humankind in the beginning. God created human beings to live in fellowship with him and obedience to him. Human beings were privileged above all the other created beings, and God gave humanity responsibilities commensurate with their privileges. As they lived in fellowship with God and acted in obedience to God, they would enjoy their unique position in God's creation.

The first human beings chose instead the pathway of disobedience. This act of disobedience diverted them—and us—onto a side road that led not to continued companionship *with* God but to condemnation and estrangement *from* God. As a result, humanity faced God's judgment. The flood was the instrument of God's judgment on humanity.

GENESIS 6:5–9

[5] The LORD saw how great man's wickedness on the earth had become, and that every inclination of the thoughts of his heart was only evil all the time. [6] The LORD was grieved that he had made man on the earth, and his heart was filled with pain. [7] So the LORD said, "I will wipe mankind, whom I have created, from the face of the earth—men and animals, and creatures that move along the ground, and birds of the air—for I am grieved that I have made them." [8] But Noah found favor in the eyes of the LORD.

[9] This is the account of Noah.

Noah was a righteous man, blameless among the people of his time, and he walked with God. [10] Noah had three sons: Shem, Ham and Japheth.

GENESIS 7:1–6

¹ The LORD then said to Noah, "Go into the ark, you and your whole family, because I have found you righteous in this generation. ² Take with you seven of every kind of clean animal, a male and its mate, and two of every kind of unclean animal, a male and its mate, ³ and also seven of every kind of bird, male and female, to keep their various kinds alive throughout the earth. ⁴ Seven days from now I will send rain on the earth for forty days and forty nights, and I will wipe from the face of the earth every living creature I have made."

⁵ And Noah did all that the LORD commanded him.

⁶ Noah was six hundred years old when the floodwaters came on the earth.

GENESIS 8:13–22

¹³ By the first day of the first month of Noah's six hundred and first year, the water had dried up from the earth. Noah then removed the covering from the ark and saw that the surface of the ground was dry. ¹⁴ By the twenty-seventh day of the second month the earth was completely dry.

¹⁵ Then God said to Noah, ¹⁶ "Come out of the ark, you and your wife and your sons and their wives. ¹⁷ Bring out every kind of living creature that is with you—the birds, the animals, and all the creatures that move along the ground—so they can multiply on the earth and be fruitful and increase in number upon it."

¹⁸ So Noah came out, together with his sons and his wife and his sons' wives. ¹⁹ All the animals and all the creatures that move along the ground and all the birds—everything that moves on the earth—came out of the ark, one kind after another.

²⁰ Then Noah built an altar to the LORD and, taking some of all the clean animals and clean birds, he sacrificed burnt offerings on it. ²¹ The LORD smelled the pleasing aroma and said in his heart: "Never again will I curse the ground because of man, even though every inclination of his heart is evil from childhood. And never again will I destroy all living creatures, as I have done.

> [22] "As long as the earth endures,
> seedtime and harvest,
> cold and heat,
> summer and winter,
> day and night
> will never cease."

The Reason for the Flood (6:5–9; 7:1–6)

Why did God send the flood? One little boy in Sunday School explained that God sent the flood "because there were a lot of dirty people who needed to be cleaned up!" That child was wiser than he realized. God sent the flood because the wickedness of humanity spread from the initial act of disobedience in the Garden until it seemed to engulf all of humanity in its madness. The biblical writer concluded that "every" inclination of humanity is "only" evil "all" the time (Genesis 6:5). With staccato crispness, these words described the cosmic dimensions of humanity's problem. Sin engulfed the earth, and a lot of dirty people needed to be cleaned up.

From God's perspective, we can explain the flood in slightly different terms. By our wickedness, humanity disappointed God. The Bible states in verse 6 and then repeats the idea in verse 7: "The Lord was grieved that he had made man on the earth." The text does not attribute vacillation to God, and neither does it suggest that God changed his mind about humanity. God simply sighed out his grief over what happened to his creation.

To put it another way, the sin of humanity broke God's heart. Sin robbed humanity of peaceful relationships with other human beings. But that is not the worst consequence of sin. Sin also robbed humanity of peaceful relationship with God. But even that is not the worst consequence of sin. The worst consequence of sin is that our wickedness broke the heart of God. "His heart was filled with pain," the Bible says (Gen. 6:6). Thus, God sent the flood not only because of the wickedness of humanity but also because of God's aversion to that wickedness. That is, the flood was the response of a holy God to an unholy world.

But one point of light shone in the midst of the dark cloud over the earth caused by humanity's sin. Even though humanity broke the heart of God, "Noah found favor in the eyes of the LORD" (6:8). As he responded to God's grace in the events that followed, Noah reflected a unique quality of faith.

Noah's faith, first of all, inspired him to trust God. In the cameo portrait of Noah in the New Testament Book of Hebrews, the biblical writer stated: "By faith, Noah built a ship in the middle of dry land. He was warned about something he couldn't see, and acted on what he was told" (Heb. 11:7, *The Message*). Noah trusted the invisible things of God rather than the visible things of the world. According to Hebrews 11:1, that is how true faith manifests itself.

Noah's faith also motivated him to obey God. The biblical writer affirmed, "Noah did everything just as God commanded him" (Gen. 6:22). Noah's faith went beyond lip service. He did what God told him to do. He obeyed God even though he did not completely understand God's strategy. He obeyed God although he saw no signs that a flood

STANDING AGAINST THE CROWD

Roger Williams (about 1603–1683), an early Baptist proponent of religious freedom, believed that civil authorities had no jurisdiction over the conscience in religious matters. That position was heretical in his day, and it embroiled him in continuous controversy.

Williams left England to escape persecution. When he arrived in Boston in 1631, however, he was soon caught up in the meat-grinder of religious persecution again. He discovered the Puritans in America did not want religious freedom for everyone, just for the Puritans. Banished from the Massachusetts Bay Colony on the charge of entertaining "dangerous opinions," Roger Williams founded the colony of Rhode Island. It provided complete religious liberty to all people of every religious persuasion and of no religious persuasion.[1]

Why did Roger Williams take this action to provide religious liberty to all? Because he understood that freedom *of* religion is only possible in a context that also provides freedom *from* religion. For that conviction, Roger Williams was willing to stand against the crowd, like Noah centuries earlier.

TO APPLY NOAH'S EXPERIENCE TO YOUR DAILY WALK

- Identify the actions in your life that lead to negative consequences
- Confess those acts of disobedience
- Develop a strategy to change those acts into positive actions
- Seek instructions from God's word as you develop this strategy
- Watch for influences around you that would divert you from this strategy

was coming. Too, he obeyed God even when confronted by the ridicule of his contemporaries.

In addition, Noah's faith enabled him to wait on God. A comparison of Genesis 5:32 and Genesis 7:11 shows that Noah was 500 years old when God began to make plans for the flood and 600 years old when God sent the flood. So here is the picture. Noah built the boat in a short period of time, and then he waited. Decade after decade Noah waited. No clouds darkened the sky. No torrents of rain fell on the earth. Nothing happened for 100 years, and still Noah waited. Finally, after all those years, God ordered Noah to enter the ark (7:1). Then for seven more days nothing happened (7:10). Yet Noah waited, because Noah was a man of faith. He knew that in God's time, God would act to fulfill his promises.

Because of the wickedness of humanity, God sent a flood on the earth. But before it came, God prepared for it by giving Noah instructions to build an ark so that he and his family could be preserved. Because Noah was a man of faith, he did what God told him to do. He built the ark according to God's specifications. Then, at the appropriate time, he entered the ark, along with his family and the animals. Why did Noah take only two of every kind of unclean animal but seven of every clean animal? (See 7:2–4.) Perhaps because Noah and his family would eat only "clean" meat during their stay on the ark, they needed more of those animals. Or, perhaps Noah would use the extra "clean" animals for sacrifice to God along the way. In either case, Noah needed more of the clean animals than of the unclean animals. With Noah, his family, and the animals safely quartered on the ark, the Bible says: "rain fell on the earth forty days and forty nights" (7:12). Only those on the ark survived.

The Result of the Flood (8:13–22)

Eventually, the waters subsided and the land dried enough for Noah, his family, and the animals to disembark from their haven of protection. A year and ten days after he gathered the animals on the ark along with his family, Noah led them off the ark (compare 7:11; 8:14). With clear skies above them and solid earth under their feet, Noah and his family rejoiced. The uncertainty of the days shut up in the ark was replaced by a new expectancy. God wanted to start over with humanity. The reality of God's grace now eclipsed the reality of God's judgment (8:14–16).

At this point, God repeated to Noah and his family the challenge he earlier gave to Adam and Eve: "Be fruitful and increase in number and fill the earth" (9:1). Potential once more marked the life of humanity. A partnership with God could again be forged. As God did at the beginning of creation, and as God would do on so many occasions in the future, God made a new beginning with Noah and his family (9:1).

Note the parallels between this new beginning with Noah and the original creation (Gen. 1—2). We see the same initiative by God, the same challenge, and the same focus on humanity as being created in the image of God (see 1:17; 9:6). Notice also the associations of this passage with God's covenant with Abraham (12:1-3). We see a similar blessing by God and a similar challenge concerning many descendants. This was a high spiritual moment in Noah's life, and so Noah marked it with a sacrifice to God (8:20–21), just as Abraham would later do (12:7).

Pictures from the Flood

The story of the flood presents a picture of humanity that we need to view on a regular basis as a reminder of both our frailty and our faith. The flood reflected humanity at our worst, for the flood was God's judgment on humanity's disobedience. Yet, the flood also reflected humanity at our best, for Noah demonstrated an unparalleled level of faith, the kind of faith that transforms behavior and inspires greatness. In every generation, we have demonstrations of how low humanity can descend and how high we can rise.

The story of the flood also presents a picture of God that we need to view on a regular basis as a reminder of both judgment and grace. The intersection of the holiness of God with the sinfulness of humanity always produces judgment. Yet, God's willingness to spare Noah and his family, and God's obvious desire to start all over again with humankind remind us that in the Old Testament as well as in the New Testament, God is a God of grace. The rainbow symbolized that message to Noah and his generation (9:13). The cross would symbolize that to all of the generations following Calvary (Romans 5:8).

Applying the Lesson to Life

This story of the flood reminds us of some important truths for today. Noah demonstrates, first of all, that sometimes we must go against the crowd in order to be obedient to God. In our day when we focus so much on consensus, we are tempted to believe the majority is always right. The story in our text is only one of many stories in the Bible that disprove that assumption.

The story in our text also dismisses the common pattern of attributing grace only to the God of the New Testament while designating the Old Testament God as simply a God of judgment. From the beginning of the Bible, we see manifestations of God's grace.

Finally, the story in our text reminds us that the evil of humanity cannot ultimately thwart the plan of God for humanity. God's transforming love is ultimately more powerful than humanity's wickedness.

QUESTIONS

1. Can you think of a specific experience in your life or in the life of someone you know when the law of consequences was clearly demonstrated?

2. Why do you think God chose Noah of all the people alive at that time to build the ark?

3. What aspect of Noah's faith is most inspiring to you?

4. What do we do today that breaks the heart of God?

5. Can you think of specific ways in which God manifested grace to you on occasions when you were disobedient?

NOTES

1. Roger Williams. (2009). In *Encyclopædia Britannica*. Accessed October 9, 2009, from Encyclopædia Britannica Online: http://www.britannica.com/EBchecked/topic/644376/Roger-Williams. See also William M. Pinson, Jr., *Baptists and Religious Liberty* (Dallas, Texas: BaptistWay Press, 2007), 49–50.

Onward with God

The five lessons in unit two, "Onward with God," trace the beginnings of God's specific focus on Israel as the way in which God would bring blessing to all people. Included in this unit are lessons on Abraham (Genesis 12; 15; 17); Sarah (Gen. 18; 21); Jacob (Gen. 25; 27; 32; 35); and Joseph (two lessons, Gen. 37—50).

Each of the biblical characters in these lessons played a significant role in the outworking of God's plan. Abraham, of course, is revered throughout Scripture for his faith in believing God's promise, especially in light of the greatness of the promise and the drastic ways in which Abraham was willing to change his life in order to follow God's leading.

The lesson on Sarah, Abraham's wife, focuses on the delightful story of her own faith. Although her faith that God would provide an heir was reluctant at first, it was no more reluctant than that of Abraham. Even Abraham, the paragon of faith, had laughed at such a thought (Gen. 17:17) and tried to persuade God to accept another as his heir (17:18).

Lesson six on Jacob shows that had God not chosen to work through Jacob the deceiver, Jacob could never have earned the opportunity for himself. Jacob's receiving God's blessing did not depend on Jacob's being perfect or deserving, either before or after receiving the blessing, and not even on his repenting of his deception. God's blessing was independent of Jacob's worthiness or unworthiness to receive it. In our achievement-oriented society, likely we do not consider it fair for God to act in this way and thus for the deceiver seemingly to be so rewarded. Does such an attitude show how little we recognize our need of God's grace?

Lessons seven and eight deal with Joseph, one of the most remarkable characters in all of Scripture. He provides an example of faithfulness in spite of temptation as well as of perceptiveness in seeing his place in God's plan and commitment in seeking to fulfill it.[1]

UNIT TWO: ONWARD WITH GOD

Lesson 4	Abraham: Following By Faith	Genesis 11:31—12:7; 15:1–6; 17:1–8
Lesson 5	Sarah: Laughing At God's Promise	Genesis 18:1–15; 21:1–7
Lesson 6	Jacob: Deception and Blessing	Genesis 25:21–34; 27:22–36b; 32:22–32; 35:9–12
Lesson 7	Joseph: Tempted But Faithful	Genesis 39
Lesson 8	Joseph: Participating in God's Purpose	Genesis 45:1–15; 50:19–21, 24

NOTES

1. All Scripture quotations in lessons 4–6, are from the New International Version. All Scripture quotations in lessons 7–8 are from the New American Standard Bible (1995 edition).

FOCAL TEXT
Genesis 11:31—12:7;
15:1–6; 17:1–8

BACKGROUND
Genesis 11:27—25:11

MAIN IDEA
By faith and in spite of his
continuing doubts, Abraham
responded to God's life- and
world-changing promise
to bless all the peoples of
the earth through him.

QUESTION TO EXPLORE
How can we believe—and
continue to believe—
when to believe seems
humanly impossible?

STUDY AIM
To summarize the role of faith
in Abraham's experience with
God and to consider instances
in which God has sustained
me in spite of my doubts

QUICK READ
God asked Abraham to do
things that were difficult and
made promises to Abraham
that seemed impossible, but
Abraham believed and lived
faithfully in spite of his doubts.

LESSON FOUR
Abraham: Following By Faith

In the popular movie *Field of Dreams*, a struggling farmer heard a mysterious voice call to him, "If you build it, he will come." Trusting the voice, although not always understanding, the farmer plowed under part of his corn field (his only source of income) and built a baseball field. There he watched ghosts play baseball day after day. All the while, his bills were stacking up, and he was in danger of bankruptcy. Yet he kept following the voice when it called in spite of the struggles he faced. The movie's final scene shows a sea of cars lined up to attend the ghostly baseball game, and we know the journey was worth the price.

Abram's journey from being the son of Terah to being the father of many nations was similar to the experiences of the struggling farmer in *Field of Dreams*. The Lord asked Abram to do something outrageous and then made a magnificent promise if Abram would obey. Abram struggled to follow God's call and had a hard time understanding how the promise could be fulfilled. But faith provided sustenance and direction to Abram's life and ultimately led him toward the fulfillment of God's great promise.

With the story of Abram, the Genesis story changes emphases. In the first eleven chapters, we find a narrative of God as Creator and the beginning of God's relationship to all of humanity. The focus narrows significantly with the introduction of Abram. The direction of Genesis turns toward one man through whom God would work to reach all people. The way God chose to bless the entire world was dependent on the faith of one man.

GENESIS 11:31—12:7

31 Terah took his son Abram, his grandson Lot son of Haran, and his daughter-in-law Sarai, the wife of his son Abram, and together they set out from Ur of the Chaldeans to go to Canaan. But when they came to Haran, they settled there.

32 Terah lived 205 years, and he died in Haran.

12:1 The LORD had said to Abram, "Leave your country, your people and your father's household and go to the land I will show you.

2 "I will make you into a great nation
and I will bless you;

I will make your name great,
and you will be a blessing.
³I will bless those who bless you,
and whoever curses you I will curse;
and all peoples on earth
will be blessed through you."

⁴ So Abram left, as the LORD had told him; and Lot went with him. Abram was seventy-five years old when he set out from Haran. ⁵ He took his wife Sarai, his nephew Lot, all the possessions they had accumulated and the people they had acquired in Haran, and they set out for the land of Canaan, and they arrived there.

⁶ Abram traveled through the land as far as the site of the great tree of Moreh at Shechem. At that time the Canaanites were in the land. ⁷ The LORD appeared to Abram and said, "To your offspring I will give this land." So he built an altar there to the LORD, who had appeared to him.

GENESIS 15:1–6

¹ After this, the word of the LORD came to Abram in a vision:
"Do not be afraid, Abram.
I am your shield,
your very great reward."

² But Abram said, "O Sovereign LORD, what can you give me since I remain childless and the one who will inherit my estate is Eliezer of Damascus?" ³ And Abram said, "You have given me no children; so a servant in my household will be my heir."

⁴ Then the word of the LORD came to him: "This man will not be your heir, but a son coming from your own body will be your heir." ⁵ He took him outside and said, "Look up at the heavens and count the stars—if indeed you can count them." Then he said to him, "So shall your offspring be."

⁶ Abram believed the LORD, and he credited it to him as righteousness.

GENESIS 17:1–8

¹ When Abram was ninety-nine years old, the LORD appeared to him and said, "I am God Almighty; walk before me and be blameless. ² I will confirm my covenant between me and you and will greatly increase your numbers."

³ Abram fell facedown, and God said to him, ⁴ "As for me, this is my covenant with you: You will be the father of many nations. ⁵ No longer will you be called Abram; your name will be Abraham, for I have made you a father of many nations. ⁶ I will make you very fruitful; I will make nations of you, and kings will come from you. ⁷ I will establish my covenant as an everlasting covenant between me and you and your descendants after you for the generations to come, to be your God and the God of your descendants after you. ⁸ The whole land of Canaan, where you are now an alien, I will give as an everlasting possession to you and your descendants after you; and I will be their God."

God's Promise and Abram's Faith (11:31—12:7)

Abram was in Haran when the call came. Haran had special significance in Abram's life. After Abram's brother (named Haran) had died some years before, Abram's father, Terah, had moved their family to Haran from Ur. They had set out for Canaan, but they chose to settle in Haran. When talking to Abram, God referred to Haran both as "your country" and "your father's household." From the use of such possessive language, we can derive that Haran had great meaning to Abram. It was from this place that God said, "Go."

God didn't even tell Abram where to go. He merely said, "Go . . . to the land I will show you." God simply told Abram to pick up and leave the home he held so dear and to keep going until he was shown a place to stop.

Lest we think God unfair, God did not tell Abram to leave his treasured home without a reason. God promised Abram that if he would faithfully obey and carry out this difficult request, he would be greatly rewarded. God's promise included several blessings.

In Genesis 12:2, God blessed Abram, saying, "I will make you into a great nation and I will bless you; I will make your name great." If we could imagine Abram hearing this for the first time, we might have seen his jaw drop as if to say, *Seriously?* We learned in Genesis 11:30 that Abram's wife, Sarai, was unable to have children. Barrenness was a hopeless condition for families of Abram's time. The family legacy of barren couples would die with them, for no one would carry on the family name. Barren women seemingly had no purpose for living. Women had no options available to them other than a career in motherhood. The couple would have no one to care for them in their old age. The only way to become a great nation and have a great name would have been to have children, and Abram's hope for children had long passed. Surely Abram wondered how God planned to fulfill such an apparently impossible promise.

God also declared to Abram, "You will be a blessing" (Genesis 12:2). However, this phrase is not a future statement in the Hebrew. The phrase is a command that would read something more like, "and *be* a blessing." While Abram would receive God's blessings, he was also called to be a person who provided blessing for other people. By this command, we can see God's promise to provide for Abram was really a promise to provide for *all* people *through* Abram.

God also promised, "I will bless those who bless you, and whoever curses you I will curse" (Gen. 12:3). God would take special care of Abram. Rather than leaving Abram's life to be governed by whatever sense of justice the world saw fit, God promised he would maintain an active presence in Abram's life, thus ensuring Abram's well-being.

God's blessing concluded in Genesis 12:3 as it had in the previous verse—with a note that the blessing on Abram would extend to all people on the earth. From the outset of God's relationship with Abram, God wanted Abram to know that everything was being done so that the entire human race might come into a blessed relationship with the Almighty God.

So Abram did what God asked. Because his wife was barren and he was supposed to become a great nation, Abram surely had questions. But he also had faith. When Abram and his family arrived in Shechem of the Canaanites, God kept his promise and showed Abram where to stop. God further promised he would one day give that very land to Abram's offspring. Although again Abram may have wondered to what offspring God was referring, we only see Abram's faith as he built an altar there to worship the God he trusted.

Abram's Doubt and God's Affirmation (15:1–6)

After leaving Shechem, Abram continued living a nomadic existence and experiencing the favor of the Lord. When there was a famine, Abram traveled to Egypt for a reprieve. Eventually, though, he was kicked out of Egypt because he lied, passing off Sarai as his sister. He feared that he would be killed if the Egyptians knew she was his wife (12:10–20). After Abram and his family left Egypt, Abram and Lot, his nephew, decided to separate because of differences between them (13:1–18). Later, God aided Abram in rescuing Lot from neighboring kings who decided to take over Sodom and Gomorrah, where Lot was then living (14:1–24).

Abram then received another visit from God, which is described in Genesis 15. In light of Abram's military victory in the previous chapter, God affirmed his protection, promise, and reward to Abram (15:1). But considering God's initial promise (12:2–3), the reward Abram expected was children and land. However, Abram and Sarai remained childless. So Abram doubted God's promise and attempted to take matters into his own hands by suggesting that Eliezer, one of his servants, might function as his heir (15:2–3).

God responded to Abram's doubt by confirming his earlier promise. Abram and Sarai would indeed have a son who would be of their own flesh and blood. Then God pointed to the stars to demonstrate how numerous Abram's offspring would eventually be (15:4–5). At that point, surely Abram would have settled for just one son, but he believed God's promise of prosperity and countless descendants.

Although Abram doubted and even questioned God, we find that he ultimately trusted and that his belief was what made him righteous (15:6). Abram was not considered righteous because he followed the law and did all the things he was supposed to do; Abram was regarded as righteous because he had faith.

Establishing the Covenant and Changing Names (17:1–8)

After Abram's faith overcame his doubt, God reaffirmed that Abram's descendants would take possession of the land in which they were currently living as nomads (15:7–21). Then Abram attempted to help God along by having a son with Sarai's maid-servant, Hagar. The son of

Abram and Hagar, Ishmael, was born when Abram was eighty-six years old (16:1–16).

Thirteen years had passed after Ishmael's birth when God appeared to Abram a third time (17:1). Abram was ninety-nine. Prior to this, God had only asked Abram to leave Haran in order to receive the promise. But God placed a new condition on Abram this time. God commanded Abram, "Walk before me and be blameless." God asked Abram to live a life in which every step was taken with attention to God's direction and moral standards. Abram was asked to live every day as he did the day he left Haran. God then affirmed his covenant with Abram a third time. As a sign of the promise, God changed Abram's name to Abraham.

In Genesis 17:9–16, God gave another sign of the covenant, circumcision. God also changed Sarai's name to Sarah. Following the giving of these signs, Abraham again doubted God and laughed at the thought that a man his age and a woman Sarah's age could bear a child. Abraham even begged God that Ishmael might become the fulfillment of the promise (17:17–18). But although God again rebuked Abraham's doubt, God promised to take care of Ishmael (17:19–22).

Abraham trusted God in spite of his doubt. He followed God's direction by circumcising himself and all the males in his household (17:23–27).

ABRAM TO ABRAHAM

This lesson is about one person who had two names. The story of Abram, later called Abraham, spans Genesis 11:27—25:11. Until the promises were reaffirmed in chapter 17, the main character of this lesson was referred to as Abram. God changed Abram's name to Abraham in chapter 17.

Name changes in the Bible often have symbolic meaning. The name Abram means *exalted father*, but God gave Abram the name *Abraham* to denote that he would become the "father of many nations" (Gen. 17:5). God changed Abraham's name as a symbol of the magnitude of the promise. Nations would come to know God through Abraham. In order for a promise that big to take place, nations would have to be developed, kings established, and land given (17:6–8). God's covenant with Abraham was for all humanity to have the opportunity to know and have relationship with God—and it all started with one man who had two names.

SLAVERY AND THE BIBLE

Abraham set out for Canaan with his wife, his nephew, their possessions, and "the people they had acquired" (Gen. 12:5). The Bible
has been used in the past to defend slavery because passages like
this one showed that the great ancestors of our faith owned slaves.
How would you respond to someone who used this passage to
justify slavery? What are some other biblical passages that can be
addressed in reference to slavery?

Later in the story, after God had fulfilled his promise and Sarah had
given birth to Isaac, God asked Abraham to sacrifice his long-awaited
and greatly-cherished only son. Abraham again demonstrated his faithfulness as he followed God's direction. He had even raised a knife to kill
his son on an altar. But in that troubling moment, an angel delivered
Isaac by calling to Abraham and pointing him toward a ram that God
had provided for sacrifice so that Isaac might be spared (22:1–14).

Implications and Actions

When Abraham was asked to do things that seemed unthinkable and
promised things that seemed impossible, he responded in faith. Abraham
modeled for us what real faith looks like.

Faith isn't always easy. As we go through life, our society tends to
teach us to think critically, analyze everything, and be suspicious. In
this kind of society, a childlike faith is difficult. Sometimes we question
God and the Bible, and sometimes we even doubt—but we can see in
Abraham's example that doubt is okay. The key for Abraham, though,
was the relationship he had with God, a relationship that always sustained him. Even in doubt, Abraham continued to listen to God and
eventually found his way to belief and faithful living.

As we come to times in our lives when questioning and doubting seem
more prevalent than belief, we must rely on our relationships with God
and continue to listen to and seek him. Doubts will surface and tough
times will come, but faith can always overcome.

QUESTIONS

1. How is Abraham regarded in the rest of the Bible? (Consider these references: Matthew 1:1; Luke 1:46–55; Romans 4; Galatians 3; Hebrews 11:8–10.)

2. What promises has God made to Christians today?

3. Does it ever seem impossible that God's promises to us will reach fulfillment? Why or why not?

4. Is it okay to doubt and question? How can doubt contribute to faith?

5. What are some times in your life when you have doubted or questioned God?

6. How has your faith sustained you in times of doubt?

Genesis 18:1–15; 21:1–7

BACKGROUND

Genesis 18:1–15; 21:1–7

MAIN IDEA

Life calls us to choose between laughing at God's promise and trusting in it so that we may laugh with joy.

QUESTION TO EXPLORE

"Is there anything too hard for the LORD?"[1]

STUDY AIM

To recall times when like Sarah and Abraham I have laughed at God's promise and other times I have trusted in it

QUICK READ

Sarah laughed when God made a promise that sounded ridiculous. Then when God actually fulfilled the promise, she joyfully laughed again at God's amazing power and provision.

LESSON FIVE
Sarah: Laughing At God's Promise

My three-year-old daughter and I were riding in the car one day when she said to me in a very excited voice, "Mom, there's a horse in the sky!" Knowing it was impossible for a horse to be in the sky, I laughed and responded, "Sweetheart, horses don't live in the sky. It's probably just a large bird." But she insisted there was a horse in the sky. When we finally stopped at a red light, I looked back toward the area of the sky she was pointing to and realized there, in fact, was a cloud shaped exactly like a horse. Once again, I laughed. This time the laughter was for my lack of belief and for how ridiculous truth sometimes sounds when it comes out of the mouth of a three-year-old.

Sarah had a similar experience with truth. God made her a promise that sounded absurd, and so she laughed. When God's outrageous promise was later fulfilled, she laughed again at her own disbelief and at the power of God to do what others may think impossible.

GENESIS 18:1–15

[1] The LORD appeared to Abraham near the great trees of Mamre while he was sitting at the entrance to his tent in the heat of the day. [2] Abraham looked up and saw three men standing nearby. When he saw them, he hurried from the entrance of his tent to meet them and bowed low to the ground.

[3] He said, "If I have found favor in your eyes, my lord, do not pass your servant by. [4] Let a little water be brought, and then you may all wash your feet and rest under this tree. [5] Let me get you something to eat, so you can be refreshed and then go on your way—now that you have come to your servant."

"Very well," they answered, "do as you say."

[6] So Abraham hurried into the tent to Sarah. "Quick," he said, "get three seahs of fine flour and knead it and bake some bread."

[7] Then he ran to the herd and selected a choice, tender calf and gave it to a servant, who hurried to prepare it. [8] He then brought some curds and milk and the calf that had been prepared, and set these before them. While they ate, he stood near them under a tree.

[9] "Where is your wife Sarah?" they asked him.

"There, in the tent," he said.

¹⁰ Then the LORD said, "I will surely return to you about this time next year, and Sarah your wife will have a son."

Now Sarah was listening at the entrance to the tent, which was behind him. ¹¹ Abraham and Sarah were already old and well advanced in years, and Sarah was past the age of childbearing. ¹² So Sarah laughed to herself as she thought, "After I am worn out and my master is old, will I now have this pleasure?"

¹³ Then the LORD said to Abraham, "Why did Sarah laugh and say, 'Will I really have a child, now that I am old?' ¹⁴ Is anything too hard for the LORD? I will return to you at the appointed time next year and Sarah will have a son."

¹⁵ Sarah was afraid, so she lied and said, "I did not laugh."

But he said, "Yes, you did laugh."

GENESIS 21:1–7

¹ Now the LORD was gracious to Sarah as he had said, and the LORD did for Sarah what he had promised. ² Sarah became pregnant and bore a son to Abraham in his old age, at the very time God had promised him. ³ Abraham gave the name Isaac to the son Sarah bore him. ⁴ When his son Isaac was eight days old, Abraham circumcised him, as God commanded him. ⁵ Abraham was a hundred years old when his son Isaac was born to him.

⁶ Sarah said, "God has brought me laughter, and everyone who hears about this will laugh with me." ⁷ And she added, "Who would have said to Abraham that Sarah would nurse children? Yet I have borne him a son in his old age."

Hurried Hospitality (18:1–8)

The day God made his promise to Abraham and Sarah started just like any other. Likely, Abraham had worked all morning and had decided to take a midday nap when the day was at its hottest—the part of the day when naps were definitely preferable to work. But this day and this nap were not like any other. During this nap on this day, the Lord once again appeared to Abraham.

The first two verses raise an issue of interpretation: did the Lord appear or did three men appear? Both choices are probably true. Verse 1 states, "The Lord appeared" and verse 2 describes Abraham looking up (or maybe *waking up*) to see three men standing nearby. The Bible often describes the Lord as appearing to people in the form of messengers. Sometimes the messengers appeared as angels, as people, or in visions or dreams.

In this passage, the Lord seemed to appear to Abraham in the form of three people. Throughout the account of these three visitors, references to the visitors change between three men, one man, and the Lord. Again, all these descriptions portray what Abraham encountered. Three men had come to visit him, sometimes one man talked for the three, and at times it was clear to Abraham that the Lord was speaking through the men or one man. However, while we know that the Lord appeared to Abraham in the form of the three men, it is not clear whether Abraham immediately knew the visitors were messengers from the Lord. Rather, Abraham seemed to have become more aware of the identity of the messengers as the visit progressed.

Abraham greeted the three visitors with great respect. He ran out to greet his guests in the same manner as others did when family members visited (Genesis 29:13; 33:4). Abraham bowed before them as one would approach royalty or someone deserving admiration. By treating the men as both family and royalty, Abraham displayed great honor for his guests.

Abraham treated the men with customary Middle Eastern hospitality. How one treated visitors, travelers, and foreigners was important in a nomadic society where families might go years without seeing anyone except one another. Abraham asked that he might offer them some water, wash their feet, and bring them something to eat if he had found favor with them (Gen. 18:3–5). He might have been concerned they were upset he had not noticed them when they first arrived.[2] Providing them a drink and washing their feet was a typical and particularly refreshing offer to hot and tired travelers.

Abraham made an understated offer of "something to eat." When the visitors agreed to his proposition, Abraham rushed around the camp to prepare a large feast. He hurried to Sarah and asked her to make bread from three seahs of flour (18:6). One seah was the equivalent of two gallons, and so three seahs of bread would have prepared far more bread than three visitors could eat. Abraham then selected one of his best calves and instructed a servant to prepare it (18:7). As the bread and meat were served with curds (something like yogurt, which was commonly served with meat), Abraham did not partake but simply stood nearby while the guests enjoyed their grand meal (18:8).

Abraham offered the best he had to the visitors. Perhaps by serving this great feast to the three visitors, Abraham was offering a worthy sacrifice to the Lord without even realizing it.

A Message for Sarah (18:9–15)

Abraham appeared to be in a hurry to provide hospitality to the visitors. Then the pace seemed to slow as the men shared their message from the Lord. Sarah had stayed in the tent while the men were eating. As a married woman, it was appropriate for her to stay out of the sight of the visitors.

The visitors asked Abraham, "Where is your wife, Sarah?" Abraham told them that she was in the tent (18:9). The question seems odd because Abraham had not told the visitors his wife's name. They also would have known she was in the tent since that is where the prepared food came from. The question seems to have nothing to do with the visitors needing to know where Sarah was, but rather it revealed something about the identity of the visitors. Because the visitors knew Sarah's name,

SARAI TO SARAH

After Abram's name was changed to Abraham (Gen. 17:5), God changed Sarai's name to Sarah (17:15). No explanation is given for Sarah's name change although God promised to bless her. Sarah would be the mother of nations, and kings would come from her. Likely, both Sarai and Sarah mean *princess*, although we do not know their exact meaning. What the name change signifies is more important. God's changing a name symbolized a promise and a transformation. Sarai had lived in barrenness and sadness, but Sarah would live in fulfillment of the promise as a mother filled with laughter.

Abraham and Sarah (who was eavesdropping from the tent) surely wondered whether the visitors were more than just common travelers.

After Abraham told them Sarah was in the tent and thus within range of their voices, the Lord announced through the messengers that Sarah would have a son by that time the next year (18:10). Abraham and Sarah were quite old (18:11). Sarah was well past the normal age when women bear children. We also learn that Sarah, whom we knew was old and barren from previous chapters, was also past menopause.[3] Again, we sense the disbelief of Abraham and Sarah as the absolute ridiculous and illogical nature of God's promise was disclosed. God did not promise to just reverse barrenness; God promised a child to a barren woman who was past menopause! It is no wonder that Sarah laughed.

Sarah was not the only one who laughed. When God had made the same promise to Abraham earlier, he too had laughed (17:17). How ludicrous to think that people this old who had lived their entire lives without children could have a son! When Abraham had laughed at God's promise, God told him his son would be named Isaac, which means "he laughed" (17:19). Now Isaac's name could be linked to his mother's laughter.

As Sarah laughed to herself at the absurdity of the Lord's announcement, she thought, "After I'm worn out and my master is old, will I now have this pleasure?" (18:12). In Sarah's thoughts, we see that there was more to her laughter than just disbelief at the irrational nature of the promise. Her disbelief expressed in laughter was also emotional. She had lived her life in disappointment and sadness without a child. In her subtle, humbled laughter, it's almost as if she said, *Really, after all this sadness, now will I finally find happiness at such an old age?*

Although Sarah remained out of sight from the visitors and didn't seem to vocalize her thoughts, the Lord asked Abraham, "Why did Sarah laugh and say, 'Will I really have a child, now that I am old?'" (18:13). The

---

LESSONS TO LEARN FROM SARAH

1. Be kind to visitors.
2. Don't get caught in a lie.
3. Don't take yourself so seriously that you can't turn your mistakes of disbelief into reasons for joy and laughter.

Lord knew Sarah's thoughts and the struggle she had in accepting the promise. So the Lord affirmed that nothing was too difficult and she would have a son at the appointed time the next year (18:14). What had been spoken for Sarah indirectly through the conversation of Abraham and the messengers, now was spoken directly to her. Realizing the words had been meant for her, she became afraid because of her reaction. She tried to lie, saying she didn't laugh. It seems odd that Sarah would try to lie to the visitors (representing the Lord) when they knew her name without being told and knew her laughter and thoughts without them being audible to the visitors. Beings with such apparently divine knowledge surely would have known she was lying. Indeed, she was rebuked in a very matter-of-fact way (18:15).

The Fulfillment (21:1–7)

God did what God promised he would do. Sarah became pregnant and gave birth at the particular time God promised. Abraham named their son Isaac. Sarah's laughter, which initially had been laughter of disbelief, became laughter of joy.

Women today have many options of careers, goals, and ways to live a fulfilled life. But women in Sarah's day had fewer options. Motherhood was Sarah's only option and thus the only way to live a full life. Sarah's life had lacked purpose and was filled with hopelessness without children. But in her old age, God had given her a child—a bundle of joy. God had revolutionized her existence by changing her hopelessness into happiness.

Sarah commented, "God has brought me laughter, and everyone who hears about this will laugh with me." Two people, Abraham and Sarah, were made promises and had laughed in disbelief. Then they laughed again when their disbelief was overcome with the fulfillment of the promise—their son named Isaac ("he laughed").

Implications and Actions

When Jesus described to his disciples that it was easier for a camel to go through an eye of a needle than for a rich man to enter the kingdom of

God, they asked, "Who then can be saved?" (Matthew 19:23–25). Jesus replied, "With man this is impossible, but with God all things are possible" (Matt. 19:26). When the Lord asked the question of Abraham and Sarah, "Is anything too hard for the Lord?" we know the answer was no. Nothing is too difficult for the Lord; Jesus affirmed this thought as truth in the New Testament. We know that all things are possible with God, but living as if we believe they are can be difficult.

Faith may involve believing in things that seem irrational, like horses in the sky. So naturally we laugh at times. But the beauty we see in Sarah's story is that God can turn even the laughter of disbelief into the laughter of joy. Our goal must be then to trust in the promises we know are from the Lord so we can experience the joyful laughter even more quickly.

QUESTIONS

1. How is Sarah regarded by the rest of the Bible? (Some references to Sarah include: Romans 4:19; 9:9; Hebrews 11:11; 1 Peter 3:6.)

2. When have you laughed at God's promises?

3. Why is it so difficult to believe that all things are possible with God?

4. How has God made you laugh with joy?

NOTES

1. Genesis 18:14.

2. Gordon J. Wenham, *Genesis 16—50*, Word Biblical Commentary, vol. 2 (Waco, Texas: Word Books, Publisher, 1994), 46.

3. Gordon J. Wenham, 48.

FOCAL TEXT
Genesis 25:21–34;
27:22–36b; 32:22–32; 35:9–12

BACKGROUND
Genesis 25:19–34;
27:1—33:20; 35:1–29

MAIN IDEA
As hard as it may be to
understand or accept, God
can choose to bless imperfect
people so that they can
accomplish God's mission.

QUESTION TO EXPLORE
What would be required
for you to believe you
are a person whom God
wishes to bless and use to
accomplish God's purposes?

STUDY AIM
To state implications for my
life of God's blessing of Jacob

QUICK READ
Although Jacob was a
deceiver, God still chose to
bless him and to use him
to fulfill the promises that
God made to Abraham.

LESSON SIX
Jacob: Deception and Blessing

Many if not most of us have received an envelope in the mail that proclaims, *You've just won one million dollars!* Like many people, I usually throw the envelope in the trash without opening it. I know that my chances of winning the million dollars are small and that the senders of the envelope are trying to entice me to buy something from them.

Sometimes though, I've wondered about the envelope. What if I really did win a million dollars? What if my lack of acceptance of the statement on the envelope cost me my winnings? Why didn't I just trust the envelope and open it?

Unlike those envelopes in my trashcan, the undeserved blessing Jacob was promised did come to fruition. Being the flaw-laden people that we are, the promises of God's blessing sometimes seem too good to be true. But people who make mistakes can accept God's blessing too—only God's blessing is worth more than a million-dollar-envelope.

Genesis 25:21–34

21 Isaac prayed to the Lord on behalf of his wife, because she was barren. The Lord answered his prayer, and his wife Rebekah became pregnant. 22 The babies jostled each other within her, and she said, "Why is this happening to me?" So she went to inquire of the Lord.

23 The Lord said to her,

"Two nations are in your womb,
and two peoples from within you will be separated;
one people will be stronger than the other,
and the older will serve the younger."

24 When the time came for her to give birth, there were twin boys in her womb. 25 The first to come out was red, and his whole body was like a hairy garment; so they named him Esau. 26 After this, his brother came out, with his hand grasping Esau's heel; so he was named Jacob. Isaac was sixty years old when Rebekah gave birth to them.

27 The boys grew up, and Esau became a skillful hunter, a man of the open country, while Jacob was a quiet man, staying among the tents. 28 Isaac, who had a taste for wild game, loved Esau, but Rebekah loved Jacob.

29 Once when Jacob was cooking some stew, Esau came in from the open country, famished. 30 He said to Jacob, "Quick, let me have some of that red stew! I'm famished!" (That is why he was also called Edom.)

31 Jacob replied, "First sell me your birthright."

32 "Look, I am about to die," Esau said. "What good is the birthright to me?"

33 But Jacob said, "Swear to me first." So he swore an oath to him, selling his birthright to Jacob.

34 Then Jacob gave Esau some bread and some lentil stew. He ate and drank, and then got up and left.

So Esau despised his birthright.

GENESIS 27:22–36B

22 Jacob went close to his father Isaac, who touched him and said, "The voice is the voice of Jacob, but the hands are the hands of Esau." 23 He did not recognize him, for his hands were hairy like those of his brother Esau; so he blessed him. 24 "Are you really my son Esau?" he asked.

"I am," he replied.

25 Then he said, "My son, bring me some of your game to eat, so that I may give you my blessing."

Jacob brought it to him and he ate; and he brought some wine and he drank. 26 Then his father Isaac said to him, "Come here, my son, and kiss me."

27 So he went to him and kissed him. When Isaac caught the smell of his clothes, he blessed him and said,

"Ah, the smell of my son
is like the smell of a field
that the LORD has blessed.
28 May God give you of heaven's dew
and of earth's richness—
an abundance of grain and new wine.
29 May nations serve you
and peoples bow down to you.
Be lord over your brothers,

and may the sons of your mother bow down to you.
May those who curse you be cursed
and those who bless you be blessed."

³⁰ After Isaac finished blessing him and Jacob had scarcely left his father's presence, his brother Esau came in from hunting. ³¹ He too prepared some tasty food and brought it to his father. Then he said to him, "My father, sit up and eat some of my game, so that you may give me your blessing."

³² His father Isaac asked him, "Who are you?"

"I am your son," he answered, "your firstborn, Esau."

³³ Isaac trembled violently and said, "Who was it, then, that hunted game and brought it to me? I ate it just before you came and I blessed him—and indeed he will be blessed!"

³⁴ When Esau heard his father's words, he burst out with a loud and bitter cry and said to his father, "Bless me—me too, my father!"

³⁵ But he said, "Your brother came deceitfully and took your blessing."

³⁶ Esau said, "Isn't he rightly named Jacob? He has deceived me these two times: He took my birthright, and now he's taken my blessing!"

GENESIS 32:22–32

²² That night Jacob got up and took his two wives, his two maidservants and his eleven sons and crossed the ford of the Jabbok. ²³ After he had sent them across the stream, he sent over all his possessions. ²⁴ So Jacob was left alone, and a man wrestled with him till daybreak. ²⁵ When the man saw that he could not overpower him, he touched the socket of Jacob's hip so that his hip was wrenched as he wrestled with the man. ²⁶ Then the man said, "Let me go, for it is daybreak."

But Jacob replied, "I will not let you go unless you bless me."

²⁷ The man asked him, "What is your name?"

"Jacob," he answered.

²⁸ Then the man said, "Your name will no longer be Jacob, but Israel, because you have struggled with God and with men and have overcome."

²⁹ Jacob said, "Please tell me your name."

But he replied, "Why do you ask my name?" Then he blessed him there.

³⁰ So Jacob called the place Peniel, saying, "It is because I saw God face to face, and yet my life was spared."

³¹ The sun rose above him as he passed Peniel, and he was limping because of his hip. ³² Therefore to this day the Israelites do not eat the tendon attached to the socket of the hip, because the socket of Jacob's hip was touched near the tendon.

GENESIS 35:9–12

⁸ Now Deborah, Rebekah's nurse, died and was buried under the oak below Bethel. So it was named Allon Bacuth.

⁹ After Jacob returned from Paddan Aram, God appeared to him again and blessed him. ¹⁰ God said to him, "Your name is Jacob, but you will no longer be called Jacob; your name will be Israel." So he named him Israel.

¹¹ And God said to him, "I am God Almighty; be fruitful and increase in number. A nation and a community of nations will come from you, and kings will come from your body. ¹² The land I gave to Abraham and Isaac I also give to you, and I will give this land to your descendants after you."

The Birth of Two Nations (25:21–34)

Isaac was the son God had promised to Abraham and Sarah. Through Isaac, God would fulfill the promises he had made to Abraham. Shortly after his mother's death, Isaac married Rebekah. She was from Abraham's family in Haran and thus of respectable lineage.

In order for the promise God had made to Abraham to be fulfilled, Isaac needed a son through whom the promise could be passed down. Again however, as with Sarah in lesson five, we encounter the problem of barrenness, for Rebekah was barren.

Isaac prayed that Rebekah's barrenness might be reversed. The word "prayed" means more than just a simple prayer. The word conveys a fervent pleading to God and often was used to ask God to change something. Isaac asked God for a child for twenty years, beginning when he was forty years old (Genesis 25:20, 26). Isaac's appeal demonstrates how powerful our prayers to God can be in transforming our reality. Rebekah was barren. Isaac prayed earnestly. God answered with Rebekah's pregnancy (Gen. 25:21).

Today, we can determine through sonogram technology that twins are to be expected. Rebekah, though, did not know what was going on inside her. All she knew was that there was quite an uproar in her abdomen. The narrator, who knew what was going to happen, revealed that it was not a baby, but *babies*, who were causing the internal ruckus. But the unaware Rebekah was greatly troubled, and perhaps pained, by all the commotion. So she consulted the Lord to find out what was going on (25:22).

WHY JACOB?

God's selection of Jacob, the son of Isaac who would receive the blessing, had nothing to do with Jacob's worth. God destined Jacob from the womb to be the heir of the promise. Although Esau was a brash hunter who did not treat his birthright with respect, Jacob was a trickster who seemed willing to deceive anyone to get what he thought he deserved. Yet, Jacob received the promise and blessing. For the deceiver to be rewarded may not seem fair.

When God chose Jacob, God upset the social order of the ancient world. By choosing the younger brother, God may have been demonstrating his concern for all people in whatever place in the social order. Throughout the Old Testament, God showed concern for widows, orphans, and those who otherwise had no social standing. We may be reminded of Jesus' statement in Matthew 20:16, "So the last will be first, and the first will be last." Perhaps Jacob was an example of such principles.

But a problem still remains. How does someone who blatantly betrays others receive God's blessing? Ultimately, God is free to choose whomever God wishes to choose. Our finite minds may never be able to understand the ways of the infinite God. We can be sure that God will accomplish his purposes for humanity through the means he deems fit and that, as God's people, we will be better off for it.

The Lord revealed that Rebekah would be having twins. On the surface, that would seem to explain the disturbance in her womb. But there was more to the story. Not only would Rebekah be having twins, but these twins were, and would continue to be throughout their lives, in conflict with each other. They would become two separate nations instead of existing as a part of one family. One would be stronger than the other. The older would serve the younger (25:23).

A younger sibling ruling over an older would have disrupted the ancient social order. Such an inversion of power just didn't happen. The older traditionally received the power, the inheritance, and the blessing. Rebekah surely kept this word from the Lord at the forefront of her mind and continued to attempt to understand it as the twins grew.

The boys were born. The first one was named Esau because he was hairy. The second came out holding Esau's heel and was named Jacob, which means *he grasps the heel* or *he deceives*. Although conflict surrounded them from the moment of their conception, we cannot lose sight of the fact that their birth was another revolutionizing provision from the Lord. Their birth moved forward the purposes of God and the fulfillment of God's promises in spite of human impossibilities.

An Impulsive Transaction Between Brothers (25:27–34)

The boys' lives were beginning to reflect the struggle that had been prophesied. As they grew up, they developed different tastes. Esau liked to hunt and be out in the open country. Jacob preferred to stay close to home. Isaac preferred Esau because Isaac liked to eat the wild game his older son hunted. However, Rebekah favored Jacob. Although the passage does not explicitly say she favored Jacob because of the prophecy, that possibility is certainly plausible.

One day, Jacob stayed in and cooked while Esau went hunting (25:29). I can imagine Esau brazenly blasting into the tent and demanding that Jacob give him some of the red stew that was cooking (25:30). Jacob immediately responded to Esau's demand, "First sell me your birthright" (25:31).

The Bible offers no evidence that Rebekah had conspired with Jacob to find a way to become more powerful than his brother. Jacob may or may not have known of the Lord's prophecy concerning his supremacy.

ESAU/EDOM

Esau's name literally means *hairy*. But Esau was sometimes known as Edom, which means *red*. He became the patriarch of a people referred to as Edom. Genesis 25:25 points out that Esau was red when he was born, and the stew Esau desired is referred to as "red" in Genesis 25:30. Esau possibly began to be known as Edom not just because he was red at birth, but also because perhaps he was red-headed or had a ruddy complexion.

Edom became a neighboring country to Israel. At times, Israel despised the Edomites. But occasionally leniency was shown to Edom in the Old Testament. An example is the Book of Job, whose pious title character was not an Israelite or a Judean, but an Edomite (see Job 1:1, Lamentations 4:21).

However, he seemingly had no hesitation to seize an opportunity to gain the upper hand over his brother when he saw one. Deception appeared to come naturally to Jacob, as his name would suggest.

Esau lamented that he was about to die and therefore didn't need the birthright anyway (25:32). After Esau swore on the transaction (25:33), Jacob gave him some bread and lentil soup. Esau ate, drank, and left (25:34a). That he left without speaking might have conveyed anger over his hastiness in making the deal, or perhaps he really didn't care about what had just taken place. Either way, Esau had treated something of great worth with disrespect (25:34b). Although the story ends by commenting on Esau's lapse in moral judgment, we can't forget that Jacob's scam was also worthy of rebuke.

Stealing the Blessing (27:22–36b)

Some time had passed, and the aging Isaac had become blind. He asked Esau to hunt some game for a tasty meal so that he might bless Esau before he died. Rebekah overheard Isaac's instructions to Esau and arranged for Jacob to trick Isaac into giving him the blessing instead. She cooked two young goats in the way Isaac liked so as to pass them off as wild game. She dressed Jacob in Esau's clothes so he would smell like

Esau. She even put goatskins on Jacob's neck and arms so he would feel hairy like Esau (27:1–17).

When Jacob went to his father, Isaac had some doubts about whether this son was truly Esau. But even though the voice sounded like Jacob's, Isaac was deceived into thinking this son was Esau by the hairy goatskins on Jacob's hands (27:22–24). After Isaac had eaten some of the food and drank some wine, Jacob kissed Isaac. The smell of Esau's clothes on Jacob further convinced Isaac that this son was Esau (27:25–27). So Isaac gave Jacob the blessing intended for Esau.

The blessing included an abundance of grain and fruit from the earth (27:28), political power over other nations (27:29a), supremacy over his family (27:29b), and protection from those who might oppose him (27:29c). Although this blessing was not identical to the one God spoke to Abraham, the same themes were present. Because of Isaac's blessing, God's promise to Abraham would continue to be fulfilled through Jacob.

Just as Jacob left, Esau arrived, expecting the blessing (27:30–31). It didn't take long for Isaac and Esau to realize what had happened. Both were infuriated. Isaac "trembled violently" (27:33). Esau shouted loudly, begging his father to bless him too (27:34). The emotions of Isaac and Esau are greatly pronounced in this passage. Anger must have boiled in them as Isaac commented on Jacob's deceitful nature (27:35) and as Esau agreed that Jacob was rightly named the deceiver (27:36). Although Esau begged that some blessing must be left for him, Isaac had little to offer other than promising that one day he would be able to throw his brother's yoke from his neck (27:37–40).

I FEEL LIKE ESAU

You may be able to imagine how Esau felt. His brother received what he felt he rightfully deserved. Although Esau deserved the blessing, his brother deceived his way into receiving it.

Have you or someone you know ever felt this way? Perhaps you did what you thought was necessary to be rewarded and then someone came along and stole your reward right out from under you. What does this story say to similar situations?

We may wonder why Isaac just didn't take back what he said to Jacob and offer it instead to Esau. It doesn't seem like that big of a deal to us. But in those times, blessing was a more powerful thing than we can understand. A blessing was not merely words spoken over someone wishing them well. A blessing was spoken to assure that a certain course of events would take place. A blessing could not be revoked once spoken. Therefore, by stealing the blessing, Jacob stole Esau's destiny. However, we have already learned from God's prophecy to Rebekah that Jacob one day would rule over Esau. Through Jacob's and Rebekah's deception, Jacob continued to fulfill the prophecy and, subsequently, *his* destiny.

Wrestling Angels, Injured Hips, and Israel (32:22–32)

Jacob was forced to flee because Esau wanted to kill him. Rebekah told Jacob to go back to her family in Haran. There he worked for his uncle, Laban, in order to marry Laban's daughter Rachel. But the deceiver himself was tricked by Laban. Seven years of work for one wife was turned into fourteen years of work for two wives. After working for the right to marry his wives, Jacob continued to work with Laban for several additional years. He eventually left to step out on his own and return home. In his journey homeward, Jacob was on course to meet Esau, and he began to fear for his life again. Jacob devised a plan to send ahead gifts of livestock for Esau in an attempt to pacify him and hopefully stay Esau's anger and stay alive (27:41—32:21).

Jacob stayed behind as the gifts were sent (32:22–23). In Genesis 32:24–25, a "man" who wrestled with Jacob until morning injured Jacob's hip. When morning arrived, the "man" asked Jacob to let him go. Jacob demanded a blessing and received one in which his name was changed to Israel, which means *he struggles with God* (32:26–28). So Jacob received another blessing!

After the final interchange between Jacob and the "man," Jacob remarked that he had seen God face to face in the encounter. God had appeared to the deceiver, blessed him again, and changed his name.

God's Affirmation of Blessing on Jacob/Israel (35:9–12)

After making peace with Esau (33:1–20), Jacob and his family eventually settled in Bethel (35:1). There Jacob had received a vision of the Lord when he was fleeing from Esau (28:10–22). Jacob cleansed his household of all other gods and built an altar to the Lord in his new home (35:2–7).

God appeared to Jacob again in Bethel and affirmed the blessing of the wrestling angel. Jacob's name would be changed to Israel. That Jacob would no longer be known as the deceiver did not alter the fact that he had received God's blessing from the moment of his conception and as the deceiver. God had chosen and blessed Jacob, using him in spite of his mistakes.

Implications and Actions

From the beginning, Jacob seemed prone to trickery, lies, and deception. But God chose him. Jacob was a part of God's plan no matter what his flaws were.

We all mess up like Jacob. Not one human being deserves God's blessing. Yet, God chooses to bless us anyway. As we enter into relationship with God through the grace provided by Jesus, we enter into the same blessing God promised Abraham, Isaac, and Jacob. We do not enter the blessing as perfect people but as human beings who struggle between serving ourselves and serving God and others.

Our task then is to accept the blessing and the responsibility that comes with it. We will still make mistakes. But regardless of our mistakes, we can be a part of sharing the blessing of God with others. As we do, maybe they can also accept that God will bless them in spite of their flaws.

QUESTIONS

1. How is Jacob regarded by the rest of the Bible? (Some references to Jacob include Malachi 1:2; Luke 1:33; Romans 9:10–13; and Heb. 11:9, 20–21.)

2. Jacob used trickery to get the birthright and blessing God had prophesied for him. If we feel our purpose is respectable, can we use any measure to accomplish that purpose? In what circumstances does the end justify the means?

3. Have you ever felt unworthy of God's blessing? How did you overcome that feeling?

FOCAL TEXT
Genesis 39

BACKGROUND
Genesis 37; 39—41

MAIN IDEA
Recognizing our place in God's purposes and remembering the trust that others have placed in us can help us to do what is right when faced with temptation.

QUESTION TO EXPLORE
How can we faithfully do what is right when doing wrong seems so easy and looks so attractive?

STUDY AIM
To identify truths from Joseph's encounter that I will apply to temptations I am facing

QUICK READ
The story of Joseph in Potiphar's house teaches us how we can overcome temptations by remembering our relationships with and commitments to God and others.

LESSON SEVEN
Joseph: Tempted But Faithful

All people have at least one thing in common; all face temptations daily. Temptations are those experiences in which we are enticed to engage in activity that violates God's plan and desire for our lives.

While the severity and specifics of the temptations vary from person to person, all temptations have this in common; they draw people's attention away from what they know to be right. They cause us Christians to forget at least momentarily the commitment we made to God and/or to another person. Once we have given in to temptation, we may more easily be drawn further away and also experience God's judgment.

Yet we believers have been given power to defeat temptation if we remember our relationship and commitments to God and others. The story of Joseph's experience in the home of Potiphar provides us with an excellent example of how we can successfully face our daily temptations.

GENESIS 39

¹ Now Joseph had been taken down to Egypt; and Potiphar, an Egyptian officer of Pharaoh, the captain of the bodyguard, bought him from the Ishmaelites, who had taken him down there.

² The LORD was with Joseph, so he became a successful man. And he was in the house of his master, the Egyptian.

³ Now his master saw that the LORD was with him and how the LORD caused all that he did to prosper in his hand.

⁴ So Joseph found favor in his sight and became his personal servant; and he made him overseer over his house, and all that he owned he put in his charge.

⁵ It came about that from the time he made him overseer in his house and over all that he owned, the LORD blessed the Egyptian's house on account of Joseph; thus the LORD's blessing was upon all that he owned, in the house and in the field.

⁶ So he left everything he owned in Joseph's charge; and with him there he did not concern himself with anything except the food which he ate.

Now Joseph was handsome in form and appearance.

⁷ It came about after these events that his master's wife looked with desire at Joseph, and she said, "Lie with me."

⁸ But he refused and said to his master's wife, "Behold, with me here, my master does not concern himself with anything in the house, and he has put all that he owns in my charge.

⁹ "There is no one greater in this house than I, and he has withheld nothing from me except you, because you are his wife. How then could I do this great evil and sin against God?"

¹⁰ As she spoke to Joseph day after day, he did not listen to her to lie beside her or be with her.

¹¹ Now it happened one day that he went into the house to do his work, and none of the men of the household was there inside.

¹² She caught him by his garment, saying, "Lie with me!" And he left his garment in her hand and fled, and went outside.

¹³ When she saw that he had left his garment in her hand and had fled outside,

¹⁴ she called to the men of her household and said to them, "See, he has brought in a Hebrew to us to make sport of us; he came in to me to lie with me, and I screamed.

¹⁵ "When he heard that I raised my voice and screamed, he left his garment beside me and fled and went outside."

¹⁶ So she left his garment beside her until his master came home.

¹⁷ Then she spoke to him with these words, "The Hebrew slave, whom you brought to us, came in to me to make sport of me;

¹⁸ and as I raised my voice and screamed, he left his garment beside me and fled outside."

¹⁹ Now when his master heard the words of his wife, which she spoke to him, saying, "This is what your slave did to me," his anger burned.

²⁰ So Joseph's master took him and put him into the jail, the place where the king's prisoners were confined; and he was there in the jail.

²¹ But the LORD was with Joseph and extended kindness to him, and gave him favor in the sight of the chief jailer.

²² The chief jailer committed to Joseph's charge all the prisoners who were in the jail; so that whatever was done there, he was responsible for it.

²³ The chief jailer did not supervise anything under Joseph's charge because the LORD was with him; and whatever he did, the LORD made to prosper.

The Setting of Temptation (39:1–6)

Joseph's life certainly had not proceeded as he had expected. He had lived the first part of his life as the favorite son of his father Jacob, but his prideful attitudes and actions had led to resentment and jealousy in the hearts of his ten older brothers. Ultimately those feelings grew until Joseph's brothers conspired to get rid of him.

As chapter 37 records, the opportunity arose one day as Joseph went to check on his brothers. They grabbed him, threw him into a pit, and considered killing him. They decided instead to sell him to a group of travelers and then to convince their father that he had been killed by wild animals. They carried out this plan when they sold him to a group of Ishmaelites on their way to Egypt. Once in Egypt, the Ishmaelites sold Joseph to Potiphar as a slave.

Joseph must have thought his future was lost. His brothers almost certainly thought they had seen the last of him. But God had other plans. Verse 2 tells the reader that, despite what Joseph might have thought as the result of being sold into slavery, "the Lord was with Joseph." God had made a covenant with Abraham concerning his descendants, and God intended to fulfill that covenant through Joseph.

ISHMAELITES OR MIDIANITES?

Some confusion exists concerning the identity of the group that took Joseph into Egypt. Most references to this group refer to them as Ishmaelites, but Genesis 37:28 and 37:36 call them Midianites. Apparently the terms were interchangeable, with "Ishmaelite" referring to their ancestral line and "Midianite" referring to their geographical home.

There are several significant connections between the Ishmaelites and/or Midianites and the Israelites. First, they were biologically related. The Ishmaelites/Midianites descended from Ishmael, Abraham's oldest son. Joseph and his brothers were descendants of Abraham through Isaac, Abraham's second son, and Jacob. Second, when Moses fled Egypt years later, he settled in the land of Midian. He married a Midianite woman and lived there for forty years.

Although Joseph was wise and successful in his work as a slave, and Potiphar's household benefited from his success, the Bible clearly indicates that Joseph's success was due to God's presence, for it uses "the LORD" five times in these six verses. However, the Bible never states that God either appeared to or spoke directly to Joseph as he had to Abraham, Isaac, and Jacob.

Joseph's success brought him greater responsibility as Potiphar promoted him to oversee his entire household. This position brought him to the immediate attention of Potiphar's wife. Joseph's work apparently required him to be in the house with the opportunity to be alone with her. Joseph's good looks and Potiphar's wife's advances created the opportunity for temptation into an adulterous relationship.

We can place ourselves in a position in which we are susceptible to temptation. Each of us knows those areas of our lives where temptations seem to be the strongest. So we should seek to avoid places where those temptations exist.

The Appeal of Temptation (39:7, 10)

Potiphar's wife soon began to entice Joseph into a sexual relationship. Consider Joseph's situation. He had been betrayed by his brothers. He had been forcefully taken from his father and homeland. He had likely spent months or years working as a slave in Egypt. He had been raised to the position of overseer and given a large degree of freedom. All of these struggles might have tempted Joseph to see a relationship with Potiphar's wife as something he deserved. Many fall into the mistaken belief that their struggles entitle them to certain freedoms or rewards.

Too, few things in life tend to lead to greater temptation than personal success. We may easily forget that our success is a blessing from God and instead see it as something we have earned.

Joseph had reason to believe that a relationship with Potiphar's wife would have remained unknown to anyone else. He was the overseer of the other servants. His work likely required that he occasionally be in the house alone with Potiphar's wife. The appeal of a specific temptation is often greatly elevated when one believes no one else would ever know. In addition, Potiphar's wife was persistent. The Bible implies that her enticement continued for a long period of time. This gave Joseph plenty of opportunity to develop a list of rationalizations about why yielding to her advances would be okay.

Temptation may come as a single all-out assault. More frequently, sexual temptation comes as subtle flirtations we can often rationalize or excuse, but which gradually lead us away from where we should be. These small enticements may seem harmless, but they cause us to forget the bigger picture of the life God has called us to live. If we fail to guard against these, we may eventually face a larger temptation we find hard to resist.

The Defeat of Temptation (39:8–9, 11–12)

Joseph consistently resisted the temptation of Potiphar's wife. According to the text, Joseph was able to resist for two reasons. First, he was always mindful of the trust Potiphar had placed in him. He recognized the risk Potiphar had taken by placing him in such a position of responsibility, and he did not want to violate that trust by taking advantage of his position. Second, Joseph recognized that yielding to the temptation would be a sin against God. Genesis never refers to Joseph acknowledging God prior to this verse. He nonetheless demonstrated he had a desire to live a life that would be pleasing to God. He remembered not only Potiphar's trust in him, but also God's expectations of him.

A number of years ago, a popular fad swept through youth groups and churches across the country. It involved wearing shirts or other items with the initials *WWJD*. The idea was to remind people to consider

---

APPLYING THE TEXT

To apply this text to your daily life

- Mentally set the boundaries you will not cross before temptation arises
- Maintain a daily focus on your relationships with God and others
- Seek to avoid situations or places in which temptation might arise
- Flee at the first sight of temptation

always what Jesus would do in any given situation and to imitate that action. While the overall idea was certainly a good one, there was one flaw, especially when it came to temptation. The flaw was that the bracelet suggested that one should ask *what would Jesus do* when confronted by temptation. The problem is that waiting until temptation arises is the wrong time to ask the question. Jesus never waited until he was tempted to determine what to do. He had clearly defined boundaries that were firmly established before temptation arose. When tempted, Jesus simply refused to cross the established boundaries. That is what Jesus would do, that is what Joseph did, and that is what each of us should do in our efforts to defeat temptation.

Finally, notice that Joseph ran away when the temptation became more forceful. Rather than stand and seek to debate his way out, he simply removed himself from the situation. So many times honest believers find themselves in the midst of sin and wonder how they allowed themselves to fall. Often it is because they thought they could stand and defeat temptation directly. While the Bible does encourage us to resist the devil (James 4:7), it also tells us to flee from youthful lusts (2 Timothy 2:22). The writer of Genesis set up a stark contrast between Joseph in chapter 39 and his brother Judah in chapter 38. Judah not only failed to resist sexual temptation, but he also willingly walked into it. Joseph fled from it. A proven way to defeat temptation is to simply run from it.

Although Joseph did the right thing and resisted temptation, the immediate results were not positive. Potiphar's wife was so insulted by his refusal that she trumped up assault charges against him and had him thrown in prison. Once again Joseph found himself far from where he had expected to ever be. He must have questioned whether God had forgotten about him. His questions would have been even more desperate since he had done the right thing and still suffered. Can you identify with Joseph at this point?

Here again the text reminds us that God was with Joseph (Gen. 39:21, 23) and brought him success. Because of God's presence, Joseph eventually had the opportunity to gain his freedom from prison by interpreting Pharaoh's dreams in chapter 41, after which Joseph was elevated to a high position within the Egyptian government. Although Joseph faced difficulties along the way, he refused to give in to temptation. God blessed him for his faithfulness, and through Joseph, touched the lives of millions of people.

Implications and Actions

The Bible is an ancient book, but it remains abidingly relevant and up-to-date. Joseph faced many of the same temptations that we face: a bent toward arrogance; the pull of sexual immorality; and the lure of self-determination.

A glance at Joseph's life shows that he both yielded to and resisted temptation. Giving in to temptation to be arrogant led to Joseph being carried off to Egypt.

That Joseph was imprisoned when he resisted the advances of Potiphar's wife shows that faithfulness to God may not always produce visible blessings. Despite the persistence of Potiphar's wife, Joseph resisted her seductions. He remembered the trust his master had placed in him and refused to take advantage of that trust. He remembered his heritage, his link to God through Abraham, Isaac, and his father Jacob. He refused to let physical desires cause him to sin and act wickedly.

Pleasing God was important for Joseph. May we possess the same longing to remain faithful to God as did Joseph.

QUESTIONS

1. How do you usually deal with temptation?

2. What steps can you take today to be able to overcome temptation tomorrow?

3. What might have happened in the story if Joseph had given in to Potiphar's wife's advances?

4. How do you feel about the fact that Joseph's actions, while correct, led to his imprisonment? Can you name times in your life when godly behavior increased your struggles?

FOCAL TEXT
Genesis 45:1–15; 50:19–21, 24

BACKGROUND
Genesis 42—50

MAIN IDEA
As we choose to live in faithfulness to God, God graciously and often mysteriously leads us in participating in the larger purpose God will bring to pass.

QUESTION TO EXPLORE
How do the circumstances of our lives and the actions we take relate to God's purposes?

STUDY AIM
To state how the events of Joseph's life fit with God's larger purposes and to consider how the events of my life fit with God's larger purposes

QUICK READ
Although Joseph's circumstances seemed to suggest otherwise, he was playing a vital role within God's plan to fulfill the promises God made to Abraham.

LESSON EIGHT

Joseph: Participating in God's Purpose

Individuals all across our nation are living fake lives. They have taken on new names and new identities. They have moved great distances and cut all ties to family and friends. They have constructed new versions of their own previous lives. These events have occurred because they are participating in the Federal Witness Protection Program. They possess knowledge or information because of prior relationships or have simply been in the wrong place at the wrong time. While their lives have been permanently altered, many deem their experience as serving a greater purpose in helping to arrest and imprison major criminals.

Joseph's experiences likely enabled him to identify with displaced persons with new names and identities. Because of the special gift he had to dream and interpret dreams, and because of his unwise use of that gift, he found himself far from home. He had few if any prospects of returning. He had been given a new name and new identity. Yet unlike those in the witness protection program, Joseph might have wondered how his current situation served any higher purpose. He knew the stories of God's promises to his ancestors, but might he have wondered what, if any, place he had in their fulfillment? The story for this lesson allows us to see that Joseph was participating in God's plan all along and that he came to realize this himself.

GENESIS 45:1–15

¹ Then Joseph could not control himself before all those who stood by him, and he cried, "Have everyone go out from me." So there was no man with him when Joseph made himself known to his brothers.

² He wept so loudly that the Egyptians heard it, and the household of Pharaoh heard of it.

³ Then Joseph said to his brothers, "I am Joseph! Is my father still alive?" But his brothers could not answer him, for they were dismayed at his presence.

⁴ Then Joseph said to his brothers, "Please come closer to me." And they came closer. And he said, "I am your brother Joseph, whom you sold into Egypt.

⁵ "Now do not be grieved or angry with yourselves, because you sold me here, for God sent me before you to preserve life.

⁶ "For the famine has been in the land these two years, and there are still five years in which there will be neither plowing nor harvesting.

⁷ "God sent me before you to preserve for you a remnant in the earth, and to keep you alive by a great deliverance.

⁸ "Now, therefore, it was not you who sent me here, but God; and He has made me a father to Pharaoh and lord of all his household and ruler over all the land of Egypt.

⁹ "Hurry and go up to my father, and say to him, 'Thus says your son Joseph, "God has made me lord of all Egypt; come down to me, do not delay.

¹⁰ "You shall live in the land of Goshen, and you shall be near me, you and your children and your children's children and your flocks and your herds and all that you have.

¹¹ "There I will also provide for you, for there are still five years of famine to come, and you and your household and all that you have would be impoverished."'

¹² "Behold, your eyes see, and the eyes of my brother Benjamin see, that it is my mouth which is speaking to you.

¹³ "Now you must tell my father of all my splendor in Egypt, and all that you have seen; and you must hurry and bring my father down here."

¹⁴ Then he fell on his brother Benjamin's neck and wept, and Benjamin wept on his neck.

¹⁵ He kissed all his brothers and wept on them, and afterward his brothers talked with him.

GENESIS 50:19–21, 24

¹⁹ But Joseph said to them, "Do not be afraid, for am I in God's place?

²⁰ "As for you, you meant evil against me, but God meant it for good in order to bring about this present result, to preserve many people alive.

²¹ "So therefore, do not be afraid; I will provide for you and your little ones." So he comforted them and spoke kindly to them.

· · · · · · · · · · · · · · · · · · · ·

²⁴ Joseph said to his brothers, "I am about to die, but God will surely take care of you and bring you up from this land to the land which He promised on oath to Abraham, to Isaac and to Jacob."

Remembering Who We Are (45:1–4)

God continued to work behind the scenes in Joseph's life to carry out God's purposes even while Joseph was in an Egyptian prison due to the false accusations of Potiphar's wife. Joseph's gift of interpreting dreams, which had been a major cause of his brothers' jealous decision to get rid of him, became an asset that led to his release from prison.

While in prison, Joseph correctly interpreted the dreams of two of Pharaoh's servants. One of these, the royal cupbearer, promised to mention Joseph's situation to Pharaoh. The cupbearer forgot his promise until, two years later, Pharaoh dreamed two dreams that no one could interpret. The cupbearer remembered his promise and that Joseph could interpret dreams. He suggested that Pharaoh consult him to interpret the dreams the Egyptian ruler was having. Joseph told Pharaoh that his dreams indicated there would be seven years of abundant crops followed by seven years of famine. Joseph not only correctly interpreted Pharaoh's dreams, but he also recommended a plan for dealing with the coming famine. Pharaoh then elevated Joseph to the position of his chief advisor and put him in charge of carrying out the plan Joseph had suggested.

When the famine struck, it was widespread, including Canaan. The famine prompted Jacob to send his sons to Egypt to get food. They did not recognize their brother Joseph when they arrived. But, because he recognized them, he was able to test their loyalty as brothers by requiring them to return home and bring back their youngest brother, Benjamin. When Benjamin came with them, Joseph had him framed as a thief and threatened to imprison him. When the others defended Benjamin and Judah offered to take his place, Joseph was overcome with emotion. He told his servants to leave and then revealed his identity to his brothers.

Sometimes we believers who are seeking to live a life pleasing to God forget our true identity. We may listen too much to what others say about us. We may occasionally take too much credit for our successes or feel defeated when things do not work out. We may lose sight of the fact that, whether we succeed or fail, God is always working out his plans. If we want to experience the real satisfaction of participating in God's purposes, we need to be aware of our true identity as God's servants. We need to remember that God is always working to fulfill his plans whether we can see how that is happening or not.

Identifying How God Is Working Out His Plans (45:5–8)

Something had changed in Joseph's perspective during the years he was separated from his family. The young boy who had so arrogantly foretold the day when his brothers would bow before him now gave God all the credit for his elevation to a position where he had witnessed the fulfillment of that vision.

How easy it would have been for Joseph to give in to the temptation to say, *I told you so*, and to send his brothers away. Joseph, however, had come to see that even the negative experiences of life can be a part of God's grander plan. This is not to say that Joseph was a robot or pawn in God's hands. God indeed has a perfect plan for each person, but God does not impose that plan on people's lives. God allows us to choose our path and then works through our choices to fulfill his purpose for us.

We may get in our minds a picture of how God might fulfill his purposes for our lives. Then when something happens that does not fit into that picture, we begin to complain or to question and doubt God. We might get focused on what we see as an inconsistency and try to work our way out of it on our own. This story of Joseph suggests that, in those situations, it is a better idea to look for how God might be working in those difficult or unusual circumstances to bring about the fulfillment of his plans. Perhaps God leads us to make an unexpected move. While we may want to resist, Joseph's story tells us we should instead ask what God may want us to do here that we could not have done where we were. Had Joseph not been in Egypt, the Egyptians would have failed to prepare for famine, and thousands of people would have suffered.

HYKSOS

During the late eighteenth century B.C., a group of non-Egyptian people took control of Egypt. These people, known as the Hyksos, were Semitic people who were ethnically related to the Israelites. This period is the only one prior to Greek control under Alexander the Great in which Egypt was ruled by non-Egyptians. It is unclear how the Hyksos were able to gain control of Egypt.

A number of biblical scholars have suggested that the events of Genesis 42—50 took place during the time of the Hyksos. The main line of reasoning is that a Semitic pharaoh would have been more likely than an Egyptian one to promote a non-Egyptian to a high position as the pharaoh promoted Joseph. Should one accept this line of reasoning, the pharaoh who did not know Joseph came after the expulsion of the Hyksos.

Inviting Others to Participate (45:9-15)

Joseph had come to realize that God's plans were greater than his own life. God had promised great things for Abraham's descendants, and that included Joseph's brothers. Joseph recognized that God had greatly blessed him in order that he might bless others. Thus Joseph not only sent his brothers home with food, but he was also able to bring them and their families to live in the best part of Egypt. He wanted them to be able to participate fully in and enjoy God's blessings. God had indeed fulfilled Joseph's childhood dream of being the leader over his brothers (Genesis 37:5–7), but he had learned that God's purpose for this was to allow Joseph to provide for his family, not to lord it over them.

God has given believers a wonderful privilege to participate in what he is doing in our world. His ultimate purpose is to bring all people into a relationship with himself. Far too often believers have seen this as a position of privilege and have sought to impose human regulations that must be met before other people can participate. God's desire is that we take the invitation he gave us and extend it to others. God's purpose for the world involves the salvation of all people, not merely those who are like *us*. Sometimes that invitation can be difficult to extend to others, especially if they have wronged us in some way. But the story of Joseph reminds us that participation in God's larger purposes calls for us to go beyond our personal feelings to bring others in.

Staying with God's Plan (50:19–21, 24)

Jacob and the rest of his family moved to Egypt, where Joseph provided for them from the resources of Egypt. They settled in the best land and enjoyed the best Egypt could offer. Jacob was reunited with his favorite son. Later Jacob would pass on his blessing to Joseph's two sons, giving them equal standing with their uncles within the family and assuring Joseph's line a double portion of the family inheritance.

Eventually Jacob died. His death greatly concerned Joseph's brothers since they feared he would now take revenge on them for how they had treated him. Joseph, though, had learned that God's purposes are far too great to be limited to a specific period of time. He also knew that once he had committed to follow God's plan, he needed to stay with it regardless of the circumstances. Thus Joseph promised not only that he would not harm his brothers, but also that he would continue to provide for them just as he had while their father was alive.

After years of serving within the church, it can sometimes be tempting to feel that we have *paid our dues*. We can feel we have come to the end or have fulfilled God's call or purpose for our life. But as long as we are

APPLYING THE PASSAGE

To apply this passage to your daily life

- Find ways every day to remind yourself of your place as God's servant
- Ask God to reveal to you how he is working in your life
- Identify one or more people whom you can invite to participate in what God is doing
- Seek out opportunities to extend the invitation
- Commit yourself daily to follow God's leading

alive, we are called to continue serving God and inviting others to join us. Through our participation in God's purposes, we have the opportunity to bless not only the lives of those around us but also the lives of future generations. Through Joseph's faithfulness to following God's plan, God fulfilled his promises to make the descendants of Abraham into a nation through whom God would bless countless generations.

Implications and Actions

Some people keep journals in which they record events, thoughts, and feelings they experience in the course of their lives. Journals can help folks sort out what God is doing in their lives. When looked at over the course of time, events that were seemingly unrelated are seen to be linked in the panorama of our lives.

Joseph's life illustrates what Paul wrote in Romans 8:28: "And we know that God causes all things to work together for good to those who love God, to those who are called according to His purpose." When times get tough, and they will, let's not lament our situation. Instead, let's remember that God is faithful to accomplish his plans for our lives. Let's pause each day and reflect on how our experiences of the day can be part of God's plan for this world.

QUESTIONS

1. What does it mean to you to be a servant of God?

2. In what specific areas of your life do you feel God is working? What lesson is God trying to teach you?

3. How can you begin to invite others to participate in God's purposes?

4. What might have happened to the larger story of Israel if Joseph had refused to forgive his brothers?

5. How can a person be sure to stay with God's plans throughout his or her life?

Our Next New Study
(Available for use beginning June 2010)

Living Faith in Daily Life

Lesson 11   Helping Children Grow   Psalm 128; Matthew 19:13–15;
                                          Ephesians 6:1–4

Lesson 12   Being Sick and Getting Well   Psalm 116; Luke 4:38–40;
                                          James 5:13–16

Lesson 13   Relying On God's Care When   John 11:17–26; Romans 8:38–39;
            We Face Loss   1 Thessalonians 4:13–18

Additional Future Adult Bible Studies

Letters of James and John   For use beginning September 2010
The Gospel of John   For use beginning December 2010
Psalms: Worshiping the Living God   For use beginning March 2011

How to Order More Bible Study Materials

It's easy! Just fill in the following information. For additional Bible study materials available both in print and online, see www.baptistwaypress.org, or get a complete order form of available print materials—including Spanish materials—by calling 1-866-249-1799 or e-mailing baptistway@bgct.org.

Title of item	Price	Quantity	Cost
This Issue:			
Genesis: People Relating to God—Study Guide (BWP001088)	$2.35	_____	_____
Genesis: People Relating to God—Large Print Study Guide (BWP001089)	$2.75	_____	_____
Genesis: People Relating to God—Teaching Guide (BWP001090)	$2.95	_____	_____
Additional Issues Available:			
Growing Together in Christ—Study Guide (BWP001036)	$3.25	_____	_____
Growing Together in Christ—Large Print Study Guide (BWP001037)	$3.55	_____	_____
Growing Together in Christ—Teaching Guide (BWP001038)	$3.75	_____	_____
Participating in God's Mission—Study Guide (BWP001077)	$3.55	_____	_____
Participating in God's Mission—Large Print Study Guide (BWP001078)	$3.95	_____	_____
Participating in God's Mission—Teaching Guide (BWP001079)	$3.95	_____	_____
Genesis 12—50: Family Matters—Study Guide (BWP000034)	$1.95	_____	_____
Genesis 12—50: Family Matters—Teaching Guide (BWP000035)	$2.45	_____	_____
Leviticus, Numbers, Deuteronomy—Study Guide (BWP000053)	$2.35	_____	_____
Leviticus, Numbers, Deuteronomy—Large Print Study Guide (BWP000052)	$2.35	_____	_____
Leviticus, Numbers, Deuteronomy—Teaching Guide (BWP000054)	$2.95	_____	_____
Joshua, Judges—Study Guide (BWP000047)	$2.35	_____	_____
Joshua, Judges—Large Print Study Guide (BWP000046)	$2.35	_____	_____
Joshua, Judges—Teaching Guide (BWP000048)	$2.95	_____	_____
1 and 2 Samuel—Study Guide (BWP000002)	$2.35	_____	_____
1 and 2 Samuel—Large Print Study Guide (BWP000001)	$2.35	_____	_____
1 and 2 Samuel—Teaching Guide (BWP000003)	$2.95	_____	_____
1 and 2 Kings: Leaders and Followers—Study Guide (BWP001025)	$2.95	_____	_____
1 and 2 Kings: Leaders and Followers Large Print Study Guide (BWP001026)	$3.15	_____	_____
1 and 2 Kings: Leaders and Followers Teaching Guide (BWP001027)	$3.45	_____	_____
Ezra, Haggai, Zechariah, Nehemiah, Malachi—Study Guide (BWP001071)	$3.25	_____	_____
Ezra, Haggai, Zechariah, Nehemiah, Malachi—Large Print Study Guide (BWP001072)	$3.55	_____	_____
Ezra, Haggai, Zechariah, Nehemiah, Malachi—Teaching Guide (BWP001073)	$3.75	_____	_____
Job, Ecclesiastes, Habakkuk, Lamentations—Study Guide (BWP001016)	$2.75	_____	_____
Job, Ecclesiastes, Habakkuk, Lamentations—Large Print Study Guide (BWP001017)	$2.85	_____	_____
Job, Ecclesiastes, Habakkuk, Lamentations—Teaching Guide (BWP001018)	$3.25	_____	_____
Psalms and Proverbs—Study Guide (BWP001000)	$2.75	_____	_____
Psalms and Proverbs—Teaching Guide (BWP001002)	$3.25	_____	_____
Matthew: Hope in the Resurrected Christ—Study Guide (BWP001066)	$3.25	_____	_____
Matthew: Hope in the Resurrected Christ—Large Print Study Guide (BWP001067)	$3.55	_____	_____
Matthew: Hope in the Resurrected Christ—Teaching Guide (BWP001068)	$3.75	_____	_____
Mark: Jesus' Works and Words—Study Guide (BWP001022)	$2.95	_____	_____
Mark: Jesus' Works and Words—Large Print Study Guide (BWP001023)	$3.15	_____	_____
Mark:Jesus' Works and Words—Teaching Guide (BWP001024)	$3.45	_____	_____
Jesus in the Gospel of Mark—Study Guide (BWP000066)	$1.95	_____	_____
Jesus in the Gospel of Mark—Large Print Study Guide (BWP000065)	$1.95	_____	_____
Jesus in the Gospel of Mark—Teaching Guide (BWP000067)	$2.45	_____	_____
The Gospel of Luke—Study Guide (BWP001085)	$4.45	_____	_____
The Gospel of Luke—Large Print Study Guide (BWP001086)	$4.85	_____	_____
The Gospel of Luke—Teaching Guide (BWP001087)	$4.85	_____	_____
Luke: Journeying to the Cross—Study Guide (BWP000057)	$2.35	_____	_____
Luke: Journeying to the Cross—Large Print Study Guide (BWP000056)	$2.35	_____	_____
Luke: Journeying to the Cross—Teaching Guide (BWP000058)	$2.95	_____	_____
The Gospel of John: The Word Became Flesh—Study Guide (BWP001008)	$2.75	_____	_____
The Gospel of John: The Word Became Flesh—Large Print Study Guide (BWP001009)	$2.85	_____	_____
The Gospel of John: The Word Became Flesh—Teaching Guide (BWP001010)	$3.25	_____	_____
Acts: Toward Being a Missional Church—Study Guide (BWP001013)	$2.75	_____	_____
Acts: Toward Being a Missional Church—Large Print Study Guide (BWP001014)	$2.85	_____	_____
Acts: Toward Being a Missional Church—Teaching Guide (BWP001015)	$3.25	_____	_____
Romans: What God Is Up To—Study Guide (BWP001019)	$2.95	_____	_____
Romans: What God Is Up To—Large Print Study Guide (BWP001020)	$3.15	_____	_____
Romans: What God Is Up To—Teaching Guide (BWP001021)	$3.45	_____	_____

Galatians and 1&2 Thessalonians—Study Guide (BWP001080)	$3.55	_____	_____
Galatians and 1&2 Thessalonians—Large Print Study Guide (BWP001081)	$3.95	_____	_____
Galatians and 1&2 Thessalonians—Teaching Guide (BWP001082)	$3.95	_____	_____
Ephesians, Philippians, Colossians—Study Guide (BWP001060)	$3.25	_____	_____
Ephesians, Philippians, Colossians—Large Print Study Guide (BWP001061)	$3.55	_____	_____
Ephesians, Philippians, Colossians—Teaching Guide (BWP001062)	$3.75	_____	_____
1, 2 Timothy, Titus, Philemon—Study Guide (BWP000092)	$2.75	_____	_____
1, 2 Timothy, Titus, Philemon—Large Print Study Guide (BWP000091)	$2.85	_____	_____
1, 2 Timothy, Titus, Philemon—Teaching Guide (BWP000093)	$3.25	_____	_____
Revelation—Study Guide (BWP000084)	$2.35	_____	_____
Revelation—Large Print Study Guide (BWP000083)	$2.35	_____	_____
Revelation—Teaching Guide (BWP000085)	$2.95	_____	_____

Coming for use beginning June 2010

Living Faith in Daily Life—Study Guide (BWP001095)	$3.55	_____	_____
Living Faith in Daily Life—Large Print Study Guide (BWP001096)	$3.95	_____	_____
Living Faith in Daily Life—Teaching Guide (BWP001097)	$4.25	_____	_____

Standard (UPS/Mail) Shipping Charges*			
Order Value	Shipping charge**	Order Value	Shipping charge**
$.01—$9.99	$6.50	$160.00—$199.99	$22.00
$10.00—$19.99	$8.00	$200.00—$249.99	$26.00
$20.00—$39.99	$9.00	$250.00—$299.99	$28.00
$40.00—$59.99	$10.00	$300.00—$349.99	$32.00
$60.00—$79.99	$11.00	$350.00—$399.99	$40.00
$80.00—$99.99	$12.00	$400.00—$499.99	$48.00
$100.00—$129.99	$14.00	$500.00—$599.99	$58.00
$130.00—$159.99	$18.00	$600.00—$799.99	$70.00**

Cost of items (Order value) _____

Shipping charges (see chart*) _____

TOTAL _____

*Plus, applicable taxes for individuals and other taxable entities (not churches) within Texas will be added. Please call 1-866-249-1799 if the exact amount is needed prior to ordering.

**For order values $800.00 and above, please call 1-866-249-1799 or check www.baptistwaypress.org

Please allow three weeks for standard delivery. For express shipping service: Call 1-866-249-1799 for information on additional charges.

YOUR NAME

PHONE

YOUR CHURCH

DATE ORDERED

SHIPPING ADDRESS

CITY

STATE   ZIP CODE

E-MAIL

MAIL this form with your check for the total amount to
BAPTISTWAY PRESS, Baptist General Convention of Texas,
333 North Washington, Dallas, TX 75246-1798
(Make checks to "Baptist Executive Board.")

OR, **FAX** your order anytime to: 214-828-5376, and we will bill you.

OR, **CALL** your order toll-free: 1-866-249-1799
(M-Th 8:30 a.m.-6:00 p.m.; Fri 8:30 a.m.-5:00 p.m. central time),
and we will bill you.

OR, **E-MAIL** your order to our internet e-mail address:
baptistway@bgct.org, and we will bill you.

OR, **ORDER ONLINE** at www.baptistwaypress.org.

We look forward to receiving your order! Thank you!